THE SECRET LIFE
OF
EDINBURGH CASTLE

Facts, Funnies and Fables

THE CADIES

First published in Great Britain in 1995. Second Edition 1999.

© Robin Mitchell,
 The Cadies/Witchery Tours,
 352 Castlehill,
 The Royal Mile,
 Edinburgh,
 EH1 2NF
 Tel: (0131) 225 6745
 Fax: (0131) 220 2086
 email: lyal@witcherytours.demon.co.uk
 website: www.clan.com/edinburgh/witchery

Also available from Cadies/Witchery Publishing:
BOOKS: *Adam Lyal's Witchery Tales* and *About a Mile.*
VIDEOS: *Adam Lyal's Royal Mile, Georgian Edinburgh, St. Andrews* and *The Ghosts of Scotland.*

ISBN 0-9522927-1-8

Printed by Bell and Bain Ltd., Glasgow

THE SECRET LIFE OF EDINBURGH CASTLE
Facts, Funnies and Fables

THE CADIES

Researched, written and compiled by:
**Gavin Wallace, Lorna McWilliams, Brien Forbes,
Robin Mitchell, Ilona Amos**

Illustrations:
**Ian Brown
Victor Annual**

Photographs:
**Harvey Wood
Historic Scotland**

With thanks to:
**Gordon Leslie, Deborah Phillips, Nick Finnegan,
Joe White, Tam McKay
Historic Scotland
National Galleries of Scotland
Scotsman Publications**

CADIES PUBLISHING

Dedicated to the Castle Warders

Contents

Foreword — vii

1 Gems from the Castle Rock — ix

2 Exits and Entrances — 11

3 With a View to a View — 19

4 Tales of Tunnels and Tattoos — 23

5 Bang on Time — 29

6 Mons Meg — 39

7 Dear Departed Doggies — 43

8 Guess Who's Coming to Dinner? — 45

9 Emblems of Mystery — 51

10 Which Castle Are We In? — 57

Glossary — 63

Staff Sergeant Tam McKay MBE, District Gunner.

Foreword

Tam the Gun

On 24 December 1748, Captain Chalmers and a company of artillery marched north from Woolwich, London, to Edinburgh, arriving on 3 February 1749. They had been on the road for forty-one days. The present-day traveller can do the same journey in four hours, and will be greeted by much the same ancient and exciting city which beckoned to those weary 18th century soldiers.

In 1749, Edinburgh Castle stood high on its volcanic rock, overlooking the closes and wynds of an Old Town thronged with chimney sweeps, cadies and ordinary folk going about their daily work. 1749 would have been a strange time in Edinburgh following the famous Jacobite Rebellion of 1745, a changing time: today Edinburgh continues to change, but its Castle stands firm.

Edinburgh Castle moves with the times too. Let's jump forward to 1861, when time guns became fashionable throughout the world. Auld Reekie was no exception, except that she decided to fire her gun at one, while the rest of the world preferred midday. The thrifty Scots, of course, had found a way of saving eleven rounds of ammunition as well as being just a wee bit different.

Whether you hail from Scotland or furth of Scotland, you will find a warm welcome in the capital. Edinburgh is legendary for its wealth of stories, many of them to be found in Adam Lyal's *Witchery Tales* and The Cadies' *About A Mile*. Now they have turned their attention to Edinburgh Castle itself. Their book is a collection of anecdotes and humourous stories about the Castle, ranging from the blood-chilling tale of the Headless Drummer to the hilarity of the American visitor who asked why the Castle was built so close to the railway station.

I have had the pleasure of working in the Castle since 1978, firing Edinburgh's famous one o' clock gun every day and meeting new people, hearing new stories, every day. The ghosts of yesteryear still haunt the Castle, and will do so until the end of time!

I could tell you an unusual story of my own about the Castle, but – oops – its five to one, and I've got to go! If you want to hear it, you'll have to read this book!

Bye!
Aye yours,

Tam the Gun
Edinburgh Castle, 1994

Gems from the Castle Rock

EDINBURGH CASTLE has played a central role in the history of Scotland for over nine hundred years. The country's most impregnable fortress has been, and continues to be, many different things. Until the 17th century it provided a safe haven for the Royal House of Stuart. It has been an equally secure State Prison, and provided a rock solid repository for Scotland's State Records and the Scottish Crown Jewels. For a long time it was the country's principal arsenal, and until relatively recently, served as infantry barracks.

As a national monument, Edinburgh Castle is truly majestic, but it is not static. Indeed, the eroded remains of the 340 million years old volcano that forms the rock on which the Castle was built is perhaps the only permanent feature of the whole edifice – and even the rock underwent a facelift in the 1960's! As a group of disparate buildings serving specific needs and reflecting changing styles and changing values, 'Edinburgh Castle' in truth is several monuments in one, heavy with the massive weight of a national history that is still happening. The rock that rises dramatically through the floor of the 20th century Scottish National War Memorial also provides the foundations of the 12th century St Margaret's Chapel. Even the mighty rock itself has been forced to yield to the pressures of late 20th century life, with a new vehicle tunnel hewn from it in the 1980s, urgently needed to segregate increasing traffic from increasing visitors.

Rock Concert, Castle Esplanade, 1993.

During preliminary excavations for this tunnel, the first evidence of prehistoric man's presence on the Castle Rock was found. No more potent symbol of Edinburgh Castle's dramatic enfolding of the past and the present could be imagined. Through that tunnel and across the Esplanade time itself flows in and out, in all directions, and it is always a busy, busy time. There are no less than eighteen separate Departments, Headquarters, Institutions and Businesses hard at work within Edinburgh Castle, every day, every week, every year. There are guided tours to organise, shops to run, guns and fireworks displays to be fired, cannons old and new to be cleaned, Tattoos with casts of thousands to be staged, rock stars and royalty to be pampered. And somebody has to clean all the windows, and put the bins out.

Pause for a moment, and consider all this frenzy of human activity in the name of history – old history, and new history. Consider the infinity of little facts, funnies and folklore which comprise the secret life of a phenomenon like Edinburgh Castle – the kind of raw material which often seems too trivial, too ticklish, or too fantastic to gain admittance to the official mound of guidebooks and chronicles which by now is bigger than the Castle Rock itself. Imagine how refreshing it would be to have a little anthology of this most austere of monuments in nice, bite-size, punchy anecdotes and snippets – attractive little gems rather than a lump of rock, all of which celebrate the silly and the strange with a perspective on history which is just a wee bit cheeky. And with lots of nice pictures, which show quite a different side of Edinburgh Castle

If you like the idea, you'll like this book!

The Jacobite Rebel Army's surprise attack on Edinburgh Castle, 1745.

Exits and Entrances

There are numerous tried and tested ways of getting into Edinburgh Castle. History suggests that besieging it is usually not very effective, very noisy, and slightly dangerous. Buying a ticket at the Ticket Office now seems to be the favoured method. Here is a collection of some famous and not so famous ingoings and outgoings, with, and without, tickets.

The Castle Esplanade, contrary to all appearances, was not built as a car park or a coach park. It dates from 1816-20 and was constructed as a parade ground for troops. It is now used as the site for the annual Military Tattoo, the occasional open-air rock concert, and as a parade ground for tourists.

1 million of them a year, to be precise. That's approximately 19,230 visitors a week, or 2,747 a day, or 343 an hour, or 5 every minute.

You will be reassured to know that the Castle Rock, estimated to be 70 million years old, is held together with glue. It was discovered in the 1960's that centuries of rain, snow, ice and tourists had seriously cracked the rock surface, making loose rocks and stones an increasing hazard to people and cars below. After two years of research, a construction company designed a special epoxide resin capable of withstanding the severest tests. For a further eight years the rock was extensively grouted with this super glue, with special high tensile rock bolts also inserted for good measure.

Just as well that the Castle rock is reasonably resilient, considering the number of vehicles which have got stuck at the main gate over the years, including a full-size coach and eight horses, a fire engine, and the Lord Provost's official chauffeur-driven limousine – eventually dislodged from the wall, but in a slightly different shape and with a bill for a few thousand pounds' worth of damage. Oops.

Near the front of the Esplanade there used to be a graveyard reserved specifically for witches. It was especially busy between the years 1590-1603. In the north-east corner you can see why. The Witches' Well marks the spot where between 1479 and 1722, an

A private of The Royal Scots, on sentry duty ("Wha daur meddle wi' me?").

estimated 300 men and women were 'worryit' – strangled and then burnt at the stake – for suspected witchcraft. James VI was so interested in the subject he wrote a book about it (*Which Witch is Which?*).

The exact distance from the Castle drawbridge to the entrance of Holyrood Palace is 1 mile, 106 yards. Somehow the 'Royal Mile' has stuck, rather than the 'Royal Mile and a Bit'.

Vague about Haig

The equestrian statue most available for close inspection in Edinburgh is the one of Field-Marshall Earl Haig, Commander-in-Chief of the British Expeditionary Forces in France and Belgium during the First World War, on the north side of the Esplanade. Perhaps it is symbolic that this famous and controversial Scottish General is invisible for the entire duration of the Military Tattoo, as he is screened off by the massive spectator stands. If the Tattoo is not on, visitors like to perch on the statue's rough-hewn stone base to pose for photographs, though not all of them appear to know who Haig was. One lady guiding a party pointed to the statue as the likeness of another military man altogether. When she was corrected, she exclaimed

"Ee luv, every time Ah've coom oop ere wi' t'coach Ah've told 'em it were Lord Kitchener!"

Anyway, you can only photograph the statue in black and white. Earl Haig was colour blind.

When you reach the gateway, you will find two soldiers on duty as a ceremonial guard during the summer months. Most visitors fail to realise that both guards are not permitted to speak. They won't even squeak if you stand on their toes or empty an ice-cream down their rifle-barrels, though trying to prove this is not recommended. If you happen to see a third soldier wandering around in a vaguely military fashion, you might try asking him the meaning of the motto inscribed on the gateway's porch:

NEMO ME IMPUNE LACESSIT

Curious visitors have been given even more curious replies to this question over the years by very bored soldiers, such as:

WEIGHT LIMIT 3 TONS
MIND YOUR HEAD
PLEASE CHECK YOUR CHANGE BEFORE LEAVING
GENTLEMEN PLEASE LIFT THE SEAT
DON'T SPEAK TO THE SOLDIERS
NO HANG-GLIDING PERMITTED

On a good day you might get the correct answer, which is:

NO-ONE ATTACKS ME WITH IMPUNITY

or to give it its customary Scots translation:

WHA DAUR MEDDLE WI' ME?

A party of young students apparently conveyed so many items from the Castle Shop for which the requisite monies had for some unaccountable reason not been tendered – stealing, to you and me – that the teacher had to bring the goods back in a laundry basket.

A Dead Moving Story

Ensign Charles Ewart, the Royal Scots Greys' hero of the Battle of Waterloo who captured the standard of the French 45th Regiment single-handed, has been buried four times. His body was discovered in Davyhulme, near Manchester, in 1938 by workmen clearing a site for a building in an old churchyard. His body was brought to Edinburgh later the same year, where it was laid on the Castle Esplanade under a large granite slab raised by the officers and men of his old regiment.

The trooper was exhumed again in 1967 to allow rebuilding of the North wall of the Esplanade, and was taken along with full military escort to be interred temporarily in the ancestral vault of Preston Hall, Ford, Midlothian. He spent the winter there and returned to his second resting-place on the Esplanade in the summer of 1968.

When last asked, the Ensign said he had no further travel plans, adding *I didnae have any travel plans when I retired tae Manchester either – that's why I retired tae Manchester – and look whit happened! Gonny leave us in peace noo? It wiz herd wurk nabbin that standard an I fancy a bit of kip. Savvy?*

Capturing the attention as you cross the drawbridge – the last, apparently, constructed in Scotland – are the statues of Scotland's two greatest national heroes, William Wallace and Robert the Bruce. In 1297 and 1314, at Stirling Bridge and Bannockburn respectively, these men scored outstanding victories for Scottish freedom against the huge armies of the Auld Enemy, England, during the Wars of Independence.

The re-internment of Ensign Ewart, 1968.

The statues were the work of sculptor Thomas Clapperton, and cast in 1929 in, er, England. . .

Edinburgh Castle, Nova Scotia?

It is somewhat surprising to discover that the easiest way to get to Nova Scotia is via Edinburgh Castle, where on the north wall at the head of the Esplanade there is a plaque commemorating the ceremony whereby the first eight baronets of the colony were empowered to take possession of their lands there in 1625.

Not a bad deal – in exchange for a dod of plain old Edinburgh earth, each baronet received an estate of 16,000 acres in a land too far away to get to.

The plaque was unveiled in 1953 at a ceremony attended by the Minister of State for Scotland, the Premier of Nova Scotia, the Governor of the Castle, the City's Lord Provost, and a host of dignitaries. They probably didn't have a clue what it was all about, either, but it's a nice plaque.

A Chapel for Margarets

The earliest architectural structure extant within Edinburgh Castle, and probably the oldest surviving building in the city, is the 11th century Chapel of St Margaret, built by King David I on a pinnacle of the rock in honour of his pious mother. The guild of St Margaret today are responsible for the preservation of this unique building. To become a member of the guild, you have to be called Margaret, and have Scottish connections. The building is still used for weddings, but you have to be a serving member of the armed forces to qualify for the privilege of tying the knot in this ancient and sacred spot. Oh, yes, and the name of your best man has to be Margaret.

St Margaret's Chapel is in fact ideal for Scottish weddings, as it only seats 20 people.

On Saturday 10 March 1906, the Edinburgh Architectural Association visited Edinburgh Castle with Hippolyte J. Blanc RSA to study the Chapel, which they described as *"the oldest complete ecclesiastical edifice of expressed character in the northern part of these islands"*. Hmm. If you want to read more, then you are directed to that great best-seller, *Transactions of the Edinburgh Architectural*

Robert the Bruce, victor of Bannockburn, cast in England.

Association, Volume V. Volume VI is even more exciting.

The Wars of Independence provided the backdrop for one of the most daring and spectacular assaults on the Castle in its history. Thomas Randolph, Earl of Moray, recaptured the Castle from the English in 1314 with a surprise attack by thirty men, who scaled the precipitous north face of the Rock, nipped over the walls, opened the gates, and let the heavies in. The English were gobsmacked.

This is no doubt why King Robert the Bruce ordered the dismantling of the Castle defences – *jings, lads, if Edinburgh Castle's such a skoosh tae get intae, we'd better pull it doon.*

Ah, what a metaphor for Scottish history. Win your own castle back, then kick it to bits.

The Castle has been besieged many, many times. The most destructive was the long siege which ended in 1573 after Sir William Kirkcaldy of Grange had held the Castle for Mary Queen of Scots for three years. It took an English army of 1500 men, 30 cannons and five batteries almost a month of heavy bombardment and destruction of much of the Castle before Kirkcaldy gave in and surrendered – only because the medieval David's Tower had collapsed into the Castle's main well, and the garrison had run out of water.

The Castle Governor Colonel Walter Dundas had clearly reflected on this precedent when he prepared the Castle against the encroaching army of Oliver Cromwell in 1650. Dundas, expecting a long siege, ordered a nice big carry-out for the lads – eighty barrels of beer, and a few tons of salmon to go with it. The siege began on 7 September, and Dundas gave in on Christmas Eve. He still had plenty supplies of powder, shot and provisions but the beer, of course, had long since run out – and there was still the Christmas shopping to do.

The last siege of any note at the Castle was in 1689, when the Duke of Gordon held the Castle in the name of the exiled James VII. This was a short and boring affair, lasting only three months. It is remembered solely for the fact that the most serious casualty was the Lieutenant Governor's cow, which was grazed by a musket shot. The cow surrendered on 14 June, and the rest of the garrison followed suit.

There have been lots of unfortunate people just as desperate to get *out* of the Castle as in, of course. The cellars and vaults have served to incarcerate

William Wallace, victor of Stirling Bridge, cast in England.

The secret entrance found by military genius Thomas Randolph, Earl of Moray.

many a naughty noble. During the Napoleonic Wars, French prisoners were kept here so long they had time to forge bank notes, make little trinkets to sell to outsiders, and pen some fascinating 18th century graffiti which can be seen to this day ("*Wellington is a wally*", etc.).

One Gallic guest was so desperate to escape that he hid himself in the prison dung barrow, and was thrown over the Castle walls along with a day or two's sewage. No wonder nobody went after him.

The Victorian Military Prison, opposite the vaults, dates from 1842, and was built as a result of reforms to the brutal tradition of corporal punishment. Depending on the offence, a miscreant soldier could receive anything between 50 to 2000 lashes from a cat o' nine tails – 1000 lashes were invariably fatal.

Don't be fooled into thinking, by the way, that the prison's showers demonstrate a new 19th century compassion for the inmates' comfort and welfare – they were added during the Second World War when the prison temporarily became barracks for squeaky-clean soldiers.

With a View to a View

Some of the amazing things you didn't know about the views from Edinburgh Castle, which are quite nice.

One of the most brilliant strategic innovations of Edinburgh Castle was the decision to build it somewhere really quite high which would give an absolutely superdooper view. No-one had thought of doing this before. The military implications of this stroke of genius have proved immense. Countless invading armies on their way to storming the defences have been so gobsmacked by the panoramic vistas on all sides that they have ground to a halt and had a jolly good look. It's easy to imagine soldiers over the ages pointing into the distance and making such comments as *Gosh, look, there's where we stopped in Perth for lunch*, or *As soon as this battle's over I'm going to take the wife and kids to that nice wee loch over there for a weekend's camping*.

While the eager soldiers thronged around the walls eager to get a better look, the Castle Garrison rushed out and gubbed them.

One military gentleman who has visited the Castle at least three times, but never seen the view, is the spectre of the headless drummer. A soldier on sentry duty in 1650 heard the slow beat of

View of Edinburgh's New Town, shortly before it was built.

19

a drum on the Esplanade. On challenging the figure he received no answer, and fired his musket. When the alarm was raised, nothing was found. The same thing happened again, and again, and even the Governor of the Castle heard the eerie noise. The apparition was taken to be a portent of impending war, and, sure enough, Cromwell's army arrived soon afterwards and besieged the Castle. After three months, the garrison surrendered.

The views from the Castle are, of course, legendary. Here's a quick guide to help you pick out the many landmarks to north, south, east and west.

North: Bits of Edinburgh. Silvery bit in the middle is the Firth of Forth. Lumpy bit behind that is Fife. Aberdour Castle, Aberdour (not visible, but quite nice). Lumpy bits in the water are islands. Shiny bits in the silvery bit are ships.

South: Bits of Edinburgh.

West: Other bits of Edinburgh; Glasgow (not visible)

East: Can't see anything for Edinburgh Castle.

You might think it's very difficult to say *Fresh Fife fish from the Firth of Forth*, but try it on a winter's morning with a haddock in your mouth.

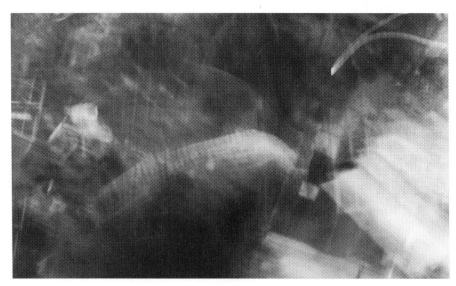

The view North, by an extremely bad photographer
(courtesy of Albert McBrien Forbes, available for weddings and revolutions).

A famous landmark is Granton Gas Works, which looks like two large soup tins floating near the shore. In 1842 Queen Victoria arrived at Granton Pier to begin her triumphant visit to the City of Edinburgh. There was nobody there to meet her from the Royal yacht, however. The Lord Provost, James Forrest, had slept in.

The clock on the tower of the Balmoral Hotel is always two-and-a-half minutes fast to act as an aid for passengers scurrying for trains at Waverley Station along Princes Street. The theory is that if they glance at this clock they will arrive at the platform with plenty of time to spare – yes, probably a couple of hours, and two-and-half minutes. . .

From the Mills Mount Battery can be seen the distinctive spire of St Stephen's Church, Stockbridge, designed by William Playfair. The clock has the longest pendulum in Europe. The clock always shows the same time because it doesn't work, so it's right twice a day. British Rail are said to be interested in the idea.

All sorts of people have attempted to scale the Castle Rock, and not just to enjoy the view the hard way. Ban the Bomb and the Scottish National Party have clambered up in protest, while two French mountaineers on holiday found the Highlands a bit tame and actually got to the ramparts, to be met by the police. A drunk managed the climb halfway, then fell off and broke his leg: he'd chosen the hardest route to climb. When the police got to him, he shouted that he'd come to save the Castle from the English. And him wi a bad leg, tae!

A couple were once found making love halfway up the rock, and more than half-naked too. Apparently they thought they had found the most private outdoor spot for the purpose, but in fact they

The Headless Drummer makes enquiries about the theft of his drum.

21

were so entirely visible that a small crowd had gathered below to enjoy the show. There was a sudden increase in visitor figures after the incident.

Aberdour Castle, Fife
(not visible from Edinburgh Castle, but quite nice).

Tales of Tunnels, Tattoos and Old Stones

The annual Military Tattoo has been held on the Castle Esplanade since 1950 and is probably the single most popular event associated with the Castle, attracting some 200,000 spectators a year. It requires almost as many performers, so it is really easy to organise. Almost as easy as digging a tunnel with a teaspoon on a rainy day with your hands in your pockets.

A Mr Arthur Elrine of Youngstown, Ohio, who was a sergeant with the 2nd Battalion of the Gordon Highlanders and stationed at the Castle in 1920-21, claimed to have discovered a tunnel under the guard room which ran for a least half a mile under the Royal Mile. He tried to reach the end of it one night, but was forced back by "the smell, the bad air and the rats" – and the rapidly disappearing contents of his hip flask, no doubt.

Now there *is* a tunnel in Edinburgh Castle. It was constructed to permit vehicular access in the 1980s by gouging through the Castle Rock itself, and led to all manner of strange discoveries. During excavations, about 16 skeletons were found, one of them, according to an archaeological expert, showing clear signs of bad toothache.

Immediately following the grim find, a Castle official telephoned the police to inform them. Before five minutes had elapsed the Castle was besieged by a convoy of police cars, vans and ambulances on full mass murder investigation alert, sirens wailing and blue lights flashing. Apparently the officer on duty who took the call raised the alarm on hearing the words . . . *16 bodies found at Edinburgh Castle*, having missed the vital qualification . . . *we think they're about 300 years old. . . Hello? Hello??*

*Popular Edinburgh Military Tattoo devotee Gordon MacMillan, 22, of Napier University,
Edinburgh, takes his seat at 4.30 am on the 27th May 1994.
His other hobbies include counting coaches.*

The new Vehicle Tunnel has breached the defences of the once virtually impregnable Edinburgh Castle forever. Since it was opened, the Castle has been repeatedly invaded by a new and stealthy enemy – squirrels.

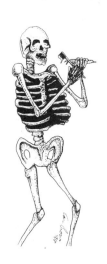

It would appear that the Castle Rock is radioactive. As part of an educational children's TV programme, a radioactive plug was concealed in part of the Rock to allow a group of nippers lots of scientific fun tracking down its whereabouts with Geiger counters. To the delight of the producer and presenter, all the junior nuclear physicists returned registering impressively high readings of radiation. To their slight consternation, it soon became apparent that the by-now gibbering Geiger counters had nothing to do with the aforementioned plug, because when they went to remove it, it wasn't there.

Watch out for the headlines: CASTLE VISITOR MAULED BY MAN-EATING MUTANT SQUIRREL.

As anyone involved in organising the annual Military Tattoo on the Castle Esplanade will tell you, never work with animals, children, or the RAF. To explain:

Once upon a time, the foreman of works was asked to prepare the Castle for the delivery of 100 horses for a Tattoo display. For six weeks he and his men worked intensively to erect stables while the blacksmith was on overtime forging iron rings and preparing to shoe some 400 horsy feet. The big day arrived, and the foremen and his sizeable team lined up to meet their prancing charges. They were just a wee bit surprised when an army lorry drove up the Esplanade, the driver jumped out, and proceeded to unload 100 wooden hobby horses. They were for a local school's contribution to the show.

Once upon a time, the foreman of works was asked to prepare the Castle for the landing of a Harrier Jump Jet for a Tattoo display. For six weeks he and his men worked extensively to erect steel beams on the coalyard roof, while a civil engineer was on overtime testing the ability of the surrounding structures to cope with the weight of the aircraft and the blast of its powerful engines. The big day arrived, and the foreman and his sizeable team lined up to await the great landing. They were just a wee bit surprised when an army lorry drove up the Esplanade, the driver jumped out, and lifted a scale-model off the trailer single-handed.

Once upon a time, the foreman of works was asked to prepare the Castle for the arrival of a Spitfire. . . and a Spitfire arrived. It was hoisted onto the coalyard roof by crane, and when the Tattoo was over it was taken down and sent back. A month later, the foreman of works was summoned to the office of the Director of Finance at the City Chambers and asked to explain the bill they had received from the RAF for £1 million. Apparently the Spitfire had never come back, so could they have the money to buy another one please?

So if you *do* know anyone with a spare Spitfire, or if you've seen one lying around, the foreman of works would just love to hear from you. . .

Approximately 2,500 macho-types are turned away from the Edinburgh Military Tattoo Ticket Office every year gravely

THE SCOTSMAN, WEDNESDAY, JULY 24, 1968

"WIZARD PRANG" ON THE RAMPARTS—Fortunately not. Despite the legendary prowess of the fighter pilot, this Spitfire was hoisted into position on the battlements of Edinburgh Castle. The aircraft has been moved temporarily from its site at the R.A.F. Station, Turnhouse, and with a Sopwith Camel, and a modern vertical take-off Harrier aircraft mounted in similar positions, will give an R.A.F. flavour to this year's Edinburgh Military Tattoo, and mark the service's 50th anniversary.

(Scotsman Publications)

disappointed to discover that Edinburgh Castle *doesn't* have a special shop where experts stencil coloured pictures of tanks, machine-guns and soldiers on your skin.

One lady was even more disappointed to discover upon reaching the Esplanade that the 45 tickets for entrance to the Castle she had bought in advance for her coach party were actually for the Tattoo. But then 'Edinburgh Castle' and 'Military Tattoo' sound so alike, don't they?

The contents of the 110 foot-deep Fore Well on the Castle's Half Moon Battery would probably finance the Tattoo for a generation.

Cleaning this 14th century water-hole out every five years or so yields an approximate 10 cwt of treasure: pennies, pounds, dollars, coinage from around the globe, trinkets, rusty watches, bottles, all by the bucket-load. One lady still regularly contacts the Foreman of Works to ask if they've retrieved her engagement ring yet, and he replies no, but we've still got dozens of wedding-rings instead, if one of those would do!

The well is thought to have a storage capacity of around 28,500 gallons. The treasure is donated to charity, though the man who goes down with bucket has been observed to have much larger pockets when he comes up again.

Children thronging around the Fore Well: "Please miss, will Tracy be able to get back up?"

A Royal Lump

The tradition of enthroning Kings on symbolic stones is one of the oldest in the world and has been used as far apart as India, Sweden and the Holy Roman Empire. Scotland's very own Stone of Destiny is shrouded in mystery, myth and legend. Some of the tales are taller than the Castle itself including the story of Jacob using the sacred stone as a pillow. I'm sure we'd all choose a lump of rock to ensure a peaceful night's sleep. Seemingly in its early career – if aspects of the tradition are to be embraced - the Stone of Destiny regularly sought out new destinations - travelling the globe from Egypt to Asia, Spain to Ireland and the West of Scotland to Scone. To miss out a large chunk of history and to cut straight to the chase, King Edward 1st of England removed the relic from Scotland in 1296. This act of hostility was akin to stealing milk out of a Scotsman's porridge bowl. There were several attempts to 'free' the stone - most notably on Christmas day 1950, when four students stole the ancient artefact from Westminster Abbey and brought it back to Scotland.
They delivered it to Arbroath Abbey nine months later.

After seven hundred years, the Stone of Destiny returned to Scotland on the 30th November – St Andrew's day 1996. HRH The Duke of York was Her Majesty the Queens representative for the occasion. A twenty-one gun Royal salute from the Mills Mount Battery at twelve-noon meant an extra long day for Tam the Gun. The Stone was paraded up the Royal Mile through a throng of cheering people. Grown adults were observed waving heartily at this lump of quarry-dressed, coarse-grained red sandstone.

The Stone of Destiny is on view in Edinburgh Castle.

Bang on Time

The one o'clock gun is fired daily from the Mills Mount Battery of Edinburgh Castle at 1300 hours precisely, except on Sundays, Christmas Day and Good Friday. The firing of the time gun has been a recognised custom in Edinburgh since it was first fired on 9 June 1861. It has been fired ever since, except during the years 1939-45, for obvious reasons.

The time gun was originally intended as an audible time signal to shipping on the River Forth. The gun used is NOT Mons Meg.

The one o'clock gun is a Q.F. 25 PDR HOWITZER MK II with a calibre of 87.6mm, a range of 13,400 yards, and a rate of fire of 5 rounds per minute. It weighs 7,335 pounds. So it's a lot heavier, and a good deal more dangerous, than a wristwatch.

Tam the Gun

As crowds of tourists wait expectantly with cameras and wristwatches at the ready, every day Staff Sergeant Tom McKay

Tam the Gun does the biz.

MBE, of 52nd Lowland Brigade, The Castle – better known as 'Tam the Gun' – checks his stopwatch with British Telecom in his quarters on the lower defences of Edinburgh Castle: the District Gunner's Office. After inspecting his uniform, Britain's only District Gunner marches up the well-worn steps of the ancient castle to the Mills Mount Battery.

At five minutes to one, he loads the 50-year old howitzer, raises the barrel, and fires exactly on the stroke of one o'clock.

A mile away across the valley separating Calton Hill from the Castle, the time ball situated on the top of the mast of the Nelson Monument drops at precisely the same time as the gun is fired. More than one visitor observing the spectacle has been heard to exclaim, "Crikey, that lad's a good shot!"

The Calton Hill time ball actually came before the gun. It was mounted on the monument in 1852 to provide an accurate time check to ships in the Firth of Forth. When the ships' crews spotted the time ball falling, they could adjust their chronometers accordingly, and decide what to have for lunch. It being a well-

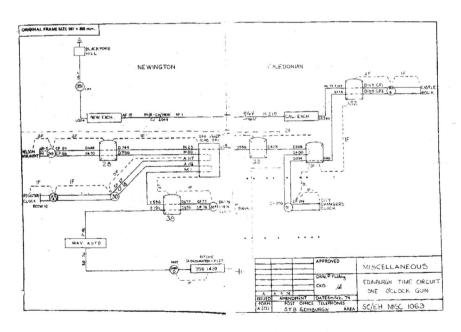

The Time Circuit of Edinburgh's One O'Clock Gun. Simple, really.

known fact that seamen are prone to short-sightedness, the city council decided that the addition of an audible time signal would be a jolly good idea as an aid to shipping, and as a means of scaring the city centre population out of their wits at exactly the same time every day.

How Not to Get A Drink in Edinburgh

To begin with, not everything went exactly according to plan. The exact time was supplied from a master clock in the observatory next to the monument. The clock for the gun was connected to Calton Hill by a steel cable 4,000 feet long and weighing 3 cwt, the longest span ever attempted in the world at that time, and an extraordinary feat of engineering. The huge cable was rigged over the roofs of the city in two days. After various tests, all was ready for the inaugural blast in June 1861. Three hundred of the capital's worthiest citizens gathered outside the observatory with one eye on the time ball, the other on the Castle, and a finger in each ear. At precisely one o'clock, the crowd held its breath. Nothing happened. The gun fuses were faulty.

The next day, the VIPs returned, confident that they would get their hands on the wine supplied for the historic occasion the day before, which was still unopened. Again the gun failed to fire: this time because the ball had not dropped down far enough to trigger the mechanism.

On the third day, a loud bang was heard from Master Gunner Finlay's field piece on the ramparts – at one o'clock precisely. Unfortunately Calton Hill was deserted, since the party had decided, after their extraordinary feat of patience, that an easier way to get a lunch time drink was to go into a pub and order one.

To this day, Edinburgh pubs are notoriously busy just before the gun goes off, carrying on a proud tradition which has been maintained in the Scottish capital since the 1860's.

The Midnight Gun is 30 Minutes Early

In 1971, the time gun was moved from the Half Moon Battery to the Mills Mount Battery, because the Half Moon Battery had been weakened by a mysterious explosion during a performance of the Edinburgh Military Tattoo on 29 August 1971. The blast destroyed the lavatories near the Wishing Well, a tea-room, a ticket-office, and damaged relics in nearby state apartments and display

Wednesday, January 9, 1946.— *The Bulletin*

FIVE BUSY MINUTES

that ensure the firing of Edinburgh's one o'clock gun dead on time. (Left) Ex-gunner Robert Thomson checks the clock by a galvanometer. (Below) He pulls up the weight, under the clock, and connects it to the lanyard that fires the gun. Next—

(Scotsman Publications)

—he loads the gun with a blank (right), and then stands by. Dead on the hour the clock releases the catch holding up the weight. It drops, pulls the lanyard and the gun fires. Out comes (bottom) the smoking shell case.

rooms. According to one expert, *if it were not for the inherent strength of the building*, the bombs could have caused a *massacre on the Esplanade.*

The explosion happened at 11.35 pm, ripping through a two-foot thick solid stone vault and two feet of concrete floor. Investigators believed that the explosion may have occurred 25 minutes earlier than intended. At midnight, the lone piper would have been standing in his spotlight high above Johnston Terrace, only feet from the explosion.

All eyes would have been turned towards the scene of the blast, and television cameras recording the Tattoo would have been trained on the building where the charges were planted. The blast actually happened during a motor-cycle display on the Esplanade, and the sound was partially masked by revving engines. It was audible even above this noise, however, and was heard as far away as Portobello.

The blast is thought to have been the work of the Scottish Liberation Army, whose exploits during the 1960s and 1970s were devoted to the fight for the independence of Scotland, and changing the time of the one o'clock gun to midnight.

Bomb damage, 1971.

When the Royal Observatory was transferred to Blackford Hill, the master-clock which sends out an electric impulse with every beat of the pendulum was installed there. The following clocks were originally included in the gun circuit: The Nelson Monument, the Main Post Office, the University Quadrangle, the time gun, and the master-clock in the premises of Messrs. J Ritchie in Leith Street, the firm who installed the original time ball. Each of these clocks could be checked on the master-clock in Ritchie's premises. At one time the gun firing mechanism was connected to the clock, and the gun fired mechanically. It is now fired manually by the gunner, who sets his stop-watch by British Telecom.

Under favourable conditions, the gun has been heard as far away as North Berwick.

Since 1867, there have been a total of 23 holders of the office of One O'Clock Gunner. The gunner from 1923-1930 is unknown.

In 1973, Dixie Deans, gunner from 1973 until 1978, was awarded a 400 per cent pay increase from £10 to £50 a year by Edinburgh Town Council. So he was still being paid less than £1 a week for his services to Edinburgh's clock watchers.

When Dixie was informed of the rise while he was at work on the windswept ramparts, he claimed to know nothing about it, saying:

What a laugh! The £10 was silly enough. The District Gunner has been paid this since 1921! I spend more than that on coffee and doughnuts trying to keep warm up here.

Tam the Gun is now the longest-serving district gunner since the tradition began in 1861, having performed the office since 1978. A certain J. Dooley held the appointment for eighteen years

One O'clock Gunners	
1867-76	Charles Adolphus Barr
1876	C.A.Barr - R.J.Spowl
1877	R.J.Spowl - John Lyon
1878	John Lyon - G. Swanson
1879	John Pitt
1880-85	A Galloughir
1885-89	Lt. J. Logie
1890-96	Sgt. Richard Roberts (Royal Artillery)
1897-98	Sgt. Robert McDougall R.A.
1899	Sgt. E.E. Sinclair
1900-01	Lt. J Harvey
1901-09	A.Dooley - R. Johnston (Leith Fort)
1909-10	A.Dooley - Lt. Ellison (Edinburgh Castle)
1910-14	A.Dooley
1914-18	W.W.I (Gun Not Fired)
1918-22	J.Dooley
1922-23	J.R.Deans
1923-30	Not Known
1930-39	Robert Thomson
1939-45	W.W.II (Gun Not Fired)
1945-47	Robert Thomson
1947-55	Peter Currie
1955-	William F. Taylor
19 -	Eddie McCarthy
19 -	GNR Paton
19 -	David Donkley
1973-78	Dixie Downs
1978 -	Ssgt. Tam McKay (District Gunner) Tam The Gun!

List of the One O'Clock Gunners, supplied by Tam the Gun.

*An artist's exceptionally bad impression of the One O'Clock Gun,
as seen from Aberdour Castle, Fife.*

from 1901 until 1919, but for the four years of the Great War, of course, didn't fire.

Tam has been on so many TV shows and featured in so many newspaper and magazine articles that he's now more famous than the gun he fires every day. He reckons he could do with a secretary to answer all the mail he receives. He's had letters addressed to:

THE ONE O'CLOCK MAN, EDINBURGH
TAM THE GUN, PRINCES STREET, EDINBURGH
TAM THE DRUM

He's amazed that they all seem to reach him safely, though as he points out, *"the ones that don't I wouldn't know about, would I?"*

The strangest TV star Tam ever appeared with was a latex sheep called Nobby, whom Tam found a much better conversationalist than Rolf Harris. During filming with the latter, at a critical moment the producer yelled CUT!, ran over to Tam, and wiped a raindrop from the famous McKay nose.

In his time, Tam has encountered many celebrities,

including the Queen, other members of the Royal Family, the daughter of Stan Laurel, and Cilla Black, who sang him a 'Cillagram' on prime-time TV. Johnny Cash once asked him if he could borrow Tam's milk. Tam buys his milk on Princes Street – a long way away – on his way to work, and was very reluctant to part with his half pint on such a cold day. Johnny Cash now takes his coffee black.

Tam hates firing the gun on a snowy winter's day, and on New Year's Day. On snowy days the force of the blast goes *right to the ground*, and is almost deafening. On New Year's Day after a good Hogmanay, just about *any* sound is deafening. Imagine what it must be like firing a howitzer with a roaring hangover. And what if it's a *snowy* New Year's Day?

(Scotsman Publications)

One of the old muzzle-loading 18-pounder guns in the Argyle Battery at Edinburgh Castle; until it was damaged, this was used to fire the one o'clock time signal for many years. As it is a very old gun, probably dating from pre-Victorian times, it may even have been the original one o'clock gun.

A roaring hangover became an ever-increasing possibility when a beer was named after the one o'clock gun. A caricature of the time conscious Sergeant was especially designed for the front of each font. He can now be in several places at once. Tam was invited to the Caledonian Brewery to sample the new ale but sadly the plant burnt down the night before his impending visit. To this day – as far as we know – Mr McKay has never tasted his own special brew and rumours of him running away from the burning inferno are exaggerated.

BLEEP

There was one special day Tam raised a glass to the heavens. The story starts on an extra busy summer's day outside the Castle cafeteria. Listening to a warder's radio, he overheard the Regimental Sergeant Major requesting the movement of military equipment. This was news to Tam, who instantly launched in to a torrent of choice army language relating to parenthood. His outbursts included the sentence, "What a **bleeping** idiot. He couldn't organise a **bleep** up in a brewery. He's a **Bleeping bleep!**" Unfortunately the warder had forgotten to take his finger off the pressel switch and Tam's rich vocabulary reverberated from every radio in the castle grounds. Subsequently, at the start of the following week, Tam was ordered to wear his best bib and tucker and parade outside the Brigadier's Office. He assumed a stern reprimand lay at the other side of the Officer's door. The Brigadier suddenly appeared waving a white piece of paper and exclaimed, "Well Tam, do you realise why you're here?" "Em.....no sir." answered Tam sheepishly.
"Well, Her Majesty the Queen is about to bestow the Most Excellent Order of the British Empire on you. What do you make of that?"
"Th.....anks." Tam was in severe shock. Blood immediately ran to his feet. As he left the office, a Major approached and asked, "What did the Brigadier want?"
When Tam explained, the Major replied, "Oh **bleep**, I suppose that rules me out for another **bleeping** year."

Tam received his MBE at Buckingham Palace, London, from Her Majesty the Queen on 28th October 1997. No choice language was used.

Mons Meg

There is of course a gun in Edinburgh Castle almost as famous as the one which goes off at one o'clock, and her name is Mons Meg. Contrary to a popular fallacy, Mons Meg is NOT the gun fired at one o'clock. Mons Meg hasn't fired since 1679.

She is the oldest surviving cannon in Europe, and with the exception of a similar siege gun at Lisbon, one of the largest ever forged. Her barrel is 13 feet long, her bore 27.5 inches in diameter, and she weighs 5 tons.

There has been controversy surrounding Mons Meg's origins. One story is that she was constructed at Carlingwark, in Galloway, and presented by the McLellans of that place to James II (whose interest in munitions is well-known) on his arrival there to besiege the Earl of Douglas in Threave Castle. Meg soon made short work of the defences, and the Castle surrendered sharpish. James was so pleased, apparently, that he granted to "Brawny Kim", the smith

Mons Meg, before restoration.

39

who made the gun, the lands of Mollance, or Monce. The smith's wife's name was Meg, hence the corruption *Mons Meg*.

Another story claims that Mons Meg was forged within Edinburgh Castle itself. The old sculptured stones built into the modern gateway of the Castle clearly show Mons Meg on her original carriage.

On Meg's current replica carriage it states that the gun was forged at Mons, Belgium, in 1486. She was a gift from the Duke of Burgundy to James II.

Meg is important because she is the only surviving example of the heaviest artillery of the fifteenth century to have a documented date of manufacture.

Records and evidence suggest that Meg could fire one of her massive granite balls up to a distance of two miles. She helped to besiege Dumbarton Castle for James III; she invaded England along with James IV; and according to Sir Walter Scott, she mounted guard at Dunnottar Castle when the Scottish Regalia was taken there for safety.

Moving Mons Meg, 1981.

Mons Meg: "I say, old boy, do you think if I fired this I could hit Aberdour Castle?"
(Scotsman Publications)

Mons Meg is always mentioned separately in military documents, testifying to the great affection with which she was regarded as one of Scotland's true heroines. On her return from England with James IV, for example, a special fee was paid to those who *brought home Monse and the other artailzerie.* Other entries state *To certain pioneers for their labour in the mounting of Mons out of her lair to be shot, and for the finding and carrying of her bullets after she was shot from Wardie Muir (near Granton) to the Castle, 10 shillings; To the minstrels who played before Mons down the street, 14 shillings; For 8 ells of cloth to cover Mons, 9 shillings,* and so on.

The Queen Bursts

Alas, the noble queen of cannons was fired for the last time when she helped to fire a royal salute to greet the Duke of York, brother of Charles II, when he came to visit Edinburgh in 1679. This time her barrel burst on firing, rendering her useless. The gunner was an Englishman, and it was rumoured in the garrison that this was no accident, but an act of sabotage. He was so jealous of the Scots having a bigger gun than the English that he overloaded Meg on purpose, meaning to do her an injury.

The bursting of Meg was only the beginning of her ignominy. After the accident she lay abandoned at the Castle for years, until she was eventually carried away to the Tower of London as an exhibit. She stayed there for seventy-five years, from 1754-1829, and might have

"Perhaps there might be a safer place to stand." (Scotsman Publications)

stayed there for good had it not been for the campaign of Sir Walter Scott. Scott petitioned George IV intensively during his visit to the capital in 1822 to give his permission for Meg's return to her rightful home, repeating the superstitious Scots saying that *Scotland would never be Scotland till Mons Meg cam' hame*. The King eventually agreed, though it would be a further seven years before the promise was carried out.

When she did finally arrive in 1829, Meg was met with a Queen's welcome. She was carried on a ship called the *Happy Janet* to Leith, then drawn up to the Castle by ten horses decked with laurels, escorted by three troops of cavalry and led by a band of pipers amidst ecstatic scenes. Until 1981 she stood proudly at the entrance to St Margaret's Chapel, when she was moved to her special home in the Castle Vaults to enjoy a well-earned retirement.

The barrel of Mons Meg is so capacious that, according to legend, several children have been conceived there – followed by a shotgun wedding?

Dear Departed Doggies

Undoubtedly, the single most important spot in Edinburgh Castle – if you are a dog – is the Dog's Cemetery, situated just below St Margaret's Chapel. If you are a dog, you will look in vain through the innumerable guides to Edinburgh Castle for some more information about this melancholy spot, since nobody seems to care a bonio about it. Man's best friend and all that, eh? Well, this is the first doggy-friendly book about Edinburgh Castle, so here you are:

Fido

It seems the cemetery owes its origins to one Fido, who had a pet owner called Colonel Barrie. When Fido passed away in 1847, a local lad was so upset that he and some friends raised enough money to bury Fido where the cemetery stands today. Sadly, there is no record of Fido's final resting-place: the stone may have been removed or become too badly weathered to read. The earliest

memorial here is dated 1886: more recently, 1998, to Bendix.

Pat

Pat, a white mongrel, owned a pet soldier called Captain St John Frame of the 72nd Highlanders. Sadly, Captain Frame was killed at the Battle of Kandahar in September 1879, so Pat began to look after his friend Major General Egerton instead. Major General Egerton, in fact, followed Pat all the way to the Egyptian campaign and helped him fight at the Battle of Tel El Kebir. Pat became so fond of the Major General that he even let him wear his many medals.

Major

Major served during the Second World War and was involved in the Normandy Landings of 1944, where he distinguished himself by many brave actions. For his valour he was awarded the Dickens Medal.

Greyfriars Bobby

Edinburgh's, if not the world's, most famous pooch is in fact not buried here, but he was known to pop up to the Castle on occasion to hear the one o'clock gun.

The doggies' gravestones were removed at one time to enable new grass to be sown. Unfortunately, someone neglected to record the precise locations of each stone, so they were rearranged according to the whim of a landscape gardener, who doubtless has mixed up for good the final resting places of Yum Yum, Tinker, Scamp, Tippy Top, Billy et. al. Why not bring in a highly-trained sniffer dog to sort out the mess once and for all?

Guess Who's Coming to Dinner?

One of the Castle's oldest buildings, the Great Hall, was built at the beginning of the 16th century. King James IV's initials 'IR4' are amongst the motifs carved on the magnificent beams of the open timber roof, though shouldn't he have written I AM 4? Anyway, the Great Hall was perhaps the only State apartment worthy of the name in the days when the Scottish monarchy resided – reluctantly – in the Castle's Palace buildings: not the most comfortable of places, for reasons easy to appreciate if you visit the Castle on a windy day.

The Hall has been used on very varied and different occasions. It was the meeting place of the Scottish Parliament until 1640, and has been the venue for some very notably political State banquets and dinners. King Charles I feasted here at his coronation on 17 June 1633, a magnificent occasion, the royal goodies served on the King's own vessels and plate, specially brought up with him from England. The precious plate was never to return, since someone had a rather novel idea on an alternative to doing the washing-up. Three weeks after the banquet, while the King was sailing on the Firth of Forth, one of his boats sank, drowning about 35 people, along with the crockery: *"his majesty's silver plate and household stuff perished with the rest, a pitiful sight no doubt to the king and the haill beholders"*. Not much of an advert for the monarchy: *"oh dear, there's my priceless china and my favourite curtains in the drink. . . oh yes, and 35 members of staff as well. . . "*

No wonder, then, that only fifteen years later, another banquet was held at the Great Hall – on paper plates – for none other than Oliver Cromwell, who was discussing, amongst other things like how difficult it is to get nice aubergines during a Revolution, how and when to put King Charles I to death.

The Black Dinner

Edinburgh Castle, towne and tower,
God grant thou sinke for sinne;
An' that even for the black dinnour
Earle Douglas gat therein

The title and the poetic curse refer not to a royal household chef who overcooked the mixed grill and paid the price, but to the days when instead of inviting your friends for dinner and saying nasty things about how they held their knife and fork after they left, you invited your friends to dinner and *did* nasty things to them with their knife and fork before they'd finished the prawn cocktail.

The event was the dastardly murder of the Douglas brothers in 1440, a deed which still casts its gruesome shadow over the assorted stains of the Castle's history. William, the young Earl of Douglas, and his younger brother David, were lured to a banquet at the Castle by the guardians of the ten-year old King James II, on the pretext of cultivating the King's friendship. In reality, the guardians were fearful and suspicious of the powerful House of Douglas as potential rivals for the Scottish crown, resting as it did on a child's head. The brothers occupied the place of honour beside the young King and a seemingly

A member of the notorious and feared Votadini Tribe, early inhabitants of the Castle Rock, beckons to some chums with his freshly baked baguette.

Visit of King Hussein of Jordan, 1966. The entire party had just sat down to an official lunch in the Great Hall when the One O'Clock Gun went off, forcing everyone to dive for cover underneath the tables. The two loyal King's bodyguards, disguised as medieval knights and standing on either side of the fireplace, stood their ground. They were too heavy to move anywhere.

pleasant and sociable banquet began. Little did they know that the plotters had already lowered the Castle's portcullis, and ensured that the rest of the Douglas retinue was too far away to present a threat to their plan.

At the end of the feast, merriment suddenly melted into terror as a black bull's head was placed before the brothers. Immediately recognising this ancient Scottish symbol – which meant that somebody present was to die – the Douglases leapt from the table and drew their swords. Dozens of vassals in armour immediately rushed in from an adjoining room, and despite the tears and howls of the boy king, the two noblemen were dragged out of the hall, given a swift trial, and beheaded. Their remains were buried within the ramparts, and an entire branch of the Douglas line was extinct.

If you are ever invited to Edinburgh Castle for dinner, don't ask for oxtail soup.

Dining in the Great Hall since then has remained the privilege of a select elite: a dinner there can only take place if a Government Minister, or the Governor of the Castle is host, the central heating is on, and it isn't the cook's day off. Here's a roll-call of some who have anxiously scanned the menu down the years for *Black Bull Head Burger and Fries (with side salad)*:

1967	Aldo Moro
1970	Association of Heating, Ventilating and Air-Conditioning Contractors
1974	Crown Prince Reza of Iran
1980	Margaret Thatcher
1983	President of the Federal Executive Council of the Socialist Federal Republic of Yugoslavia
1984	Delegation from the USSR Supreme Soviet (cancelled)
1985	President of the Republic of Cameroon
1985	Premier of the State Council of the People's Republic of China
1985	Secretary General of the Hungarian Socialist Working Party
1987	Prime Minister of the Islamic Republic of Pakistan
1990	Speaker of the Indian Parliament
1990	Crown Prince Frederick of Denmark
1992	EC Summit
1999	Tam the Gun eats his haggis sandwiches at the back of the hall

Gorbachev and the Supreme Soviet had to cancel their State Banquet in 1984 for some fifty guests because of a political emergency in Russia which forced Gorbachev to return home in a hurry. Question: what do you do with a State Banquet for 50 which nobody wants? Answer: invite a local old people's home.

The senior citizens took the place of the most powerful men in Russia, and probably had a much better time. They had better manners, too. Apparently, after the soup course was finished, the guests automatically stacked up all the empty bowls, passed them to the end of the tables, and took them over to the kitchen hatch!

After their arrival at the Castle for a State Banquet, certain members of the delegation from a certain country retired to a private room.

Meanwhile, in the rest of the Castle, a routine security check by the police with sniffer dogs was taking place. One dog kept returning

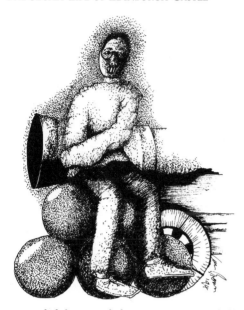

Hannibal the Cannibal sitting on a cannonball.

to the same door, scratching, sniffing, snarling and woofing itself into a frenzy. The police understandably panicked and opened the door, to find the aforementioned delegation members inside smoking several large joints.

By the time the police had made a quick diplomatic apology and left, the dog was stoned as well.

You might wonder how so many of the Great Hall's dark and amusing secrets have become such common knowledge. Easy: look high up on the right-hand of the fireplace, and you may be able to spot the *luggie-hole* or peep-hole, which has proved more than useful throughout centuries of plot and counter plot. Unfortunately, just what *really* happened at that Dinner for the Association of Heating, Ventilating and Air-Conditioning Contractors in 1970 is not fit for print.

Famous Visitors to the Castle, Dinner not Included

Burt Lancaster; William Conrad; Dolly Parton; Kenny Rogers; Rab C. Nesbitt; Anita Harris; Harry Secombe; Cilla Black; Bette Davis (particularly fascinated by Mary Queen of Scots apartments – her favourite historical character. She was accompanied by a man wearing an extremely loud tartan jacket, whom the warder assumed was her secretary. It was actually Robert Wagner); Shirley MacLean; Anthony Hopkins (just after the release of *Silence of the Lambs* – he almost caused an innocent bystander, somewhat surprised to encounter Hannibal the Cannibal in the Castle vaults, a cardiac arrest); Billy Connolly.

Famous People Who have Never Visited Edinburgh Castle

Attila the Hun; Shakespeare; Madonna; Tin-Tin; Mr Blobby; Frederick the Great; Beethoven; Enid Blyton; Saddam Hussein; Jimi Hendrix; Moses.

Emblems of Mystery

Two of the most famous – and fabulous – tales from Edinburgh Castle, both closely connected with the Scottish Royalty. Famous, but worth telling again.

What Happened on 19 June 1566?

"My Lord, God has given you and me a son – this is the son who I hope shall first unite the two kingdoms of Scotland and England". With these words Mary, Queen of Scots greeted her husband Lord Darnley as a nurse passed the new-born infant into his arms. Only a few weeks before, Mary's Italian Secretary Rizzio had been savagely murdered in her presence at Holyrood Palace, a deed in which Darnley himself was heavily implicated. It is little wonder, then, that so much controversy has come to surround the birth of the infant king in the Royal apartments of the Castle.

The discovery, in 1830, of the remains of a baby in a casket concealed within a wall in Mary's ante-room is well-documented. The remains were wrapped in a thick cloth, and within this were the decayed fragments of a richly-embroidered silk covering with two initials worked upon it, one of them distinctly I. Orders were quickly given that the casket should be closed and replaced before investigations into the body's identity could be carried out.

Rumours have been rife ever since that the immured infant's body is that of the stillborn heir to the Stuart line, and that the child who fulfilled Mary's prophecy to become King James VI of Scotland and King James I

Mary, Queen of Scots, about to enjoy the delights of a dry-roasted peanut for the first time.

Queen Mary's Room. (National Galleries of Scotland)

of Scotland and England was a 'changeling' – substituted after the true heir's death. The fabulous story certainly corresponds with another set of myths which have arisen surrounding the birth concerning babies lowered, or raised, from Castle windows; or with the belief that Mary gave birth to twins, one of whom died.

Fact or fiction? Suffice to say that if you happen to look out of the window of Queen Mary's room today, the chances of spotting a flying pig or two – with babies on their backs – are pretty high.

Honours Lost and Honours Found

Of all the stories associated with Edinburgh Castle, the tale surrounding the preservation of the Scottish Regalia – the Honours of Scotland – is the very stuff of epic heroism and romance. The jewels had been dusted down after eighteen years of disuse to be produced at the coronation of Charles II in Scone Palace in 1651: the last coronation to take place in Scotland, and an act proclaiming Scotland's defiance of Cromwell's revolution.

Cromwell, who had invaded Scotland in 1650, was determined to deal with the Scottish Crown jewels in the same way he had dealt with those of England – by destroying them. After Charles' coronation, the jewels were conveyed to the fortress of Dunnottar Castle in the east of Scotland by the Earl Marischal. Cromwell's army laid siege to the Castle for eight long months, necessitating the daring removal of the Honours to another hiding place. There are various accounts of how this was done. The jewels may have been lowered from the castle rock and hidden underneath seaweed.

Another story claims that two women carried the Regalia out of Dunnottar concealed beneath bundles of flax, right under the noses of the enemy – and that an English soldier actually helped one of the rescuers on to her horse.

However it was done, the Honours found their way to the ancient Kinneff Church, where they were buried beneath the floor, to remain there for a further nine years. After the Restoration of 1660, the Honours were restored ceremoniously to Edinburgh Castle.

A clause in the Treaty of Union between Scotland and England in 1707 declared that the Scottish crown jewels were never again to be used. Fearful of their removal to England, or Jacobite plots, the jewels were secreted into a huge oak chest and concealed within one of the walls of the Castle Crown Room.

And there they languished for over a hundred years, until the ever-vigilant Walter Scott came across a deposition in the Signet Library which revealed their whereabouts. In the long years of the Honours' invisibility, rumours had spread that this most precious symbol of Scotland's nationality had long since been stolen or removed. When George IV sent an order to Scotland stating that the room was to be opened and the truth to be made known, there

"Gosh, look what we found in the Castle wall!"

Discovery of the Honours of Scotland, February 1818: sketch by David Wilkie.
(National Galleries of Scotland)

was intense excitement in the city – and even more intense relief when, beneath a century of dust and some old linen cloth, crown, sword and sceptre were found on 17 February 1818, exactly as they had been left in 1707, and none the worse for their concealment. Soon the whole of Scotland was rejoicing at the rediscovery of these ancient emblems of the country's history.

Twice Hidden, Once Lost

Following the outbreak of war in 1939, the Honours were hidden again beneath the Crown Room for fear of aerial bombardment. By 1941, as German invasion began to seem a very real threat, the Honours were even more thoroughly concealed in the ruins of David's Tower, the medieval tower house entombed beneath the Half-Moon Battery. Plans indicating the location were sealed in envelopes and sent with utmost secrecy to His Majesty King George VI, The Secretary of State for Scotland, The King's and Lords' Treasurer's Remembrancer, and the Governor General of Canada.

When the War ended in 1945, plans were made to unearth the jewels and restore them to public display. Four very important men were heard to say *"Now, where did I put that envelope. . . ?"*

No Touch, No Go

"How much are they worth?" is the question the Warder of the Regalia expects to hear at least a dozen times a day as visitors file past the crown, sceptre, and sword lying in their cushioned, impenetrable glass case. He has a well-practised answer: *"Exactly the price of your heritage"*.

In other words, priceless. That's why there are 10-ton, safe-type Chubb doors at each of the room's points of entry, including the window. The main entrance from the courtyard steps is reinforced with a dungeon-like cross-barred door built in the 15th century to withstand a battering-ram. So the Honours are unlikely to go walkies again.

A certain Crown Prince from the Middle East visited the Honours, accompanied by his wife and three bodyguards. The wife was a spectacularly gorgeous lady, wearing a suitably glamorous ankle-length mink coat, of richly contrasting hues.

After his explanation of the displays, the warder could not resist asking about this amazingly voluptuous coat. He was informed by the Prince that it was one of their country's national treasures, and only worn on state occasions, otherwise as safely guarded as Scotland's crown jewels. There was one bodyguard for the Prince, one for his wife – and one for the coat!

One notable visitor who was particularly fascinated by the jewels – which, let's

"What Crown Jewels?"

remember, are older than those in the Tower of London and the oldest complete regalia in Europe – was Liz Taylor. After the death of Richard Burton, she came to Britain to retreat from the press, and a hush-hush visit to the Castle was arranged for her by the Directors of the Edinburgh Festival. So mesmerised was she by the Honours that virtually every gem was explained to her in great detail.

Which Castle Are We In?

Incredible, but true: this is the question the Castle Warders are most frequently asked. Let's face it, Edinburgh Castle is a pretty complicated place, and as for Scottish history – well, that's almost as slippery and treacherous to understand as the Castle Rock is to climb. So out of 1 million visitors per year, the probability of the odd goof question, the dumb remark, or just a glimpse of good old human stupidity is on the high side. As you read our concluding catalogue of gaffs, pratfalls and faux-pas eccentric, hilarious, weird and wonderful, spare a thought for the integrity and endurance of the wonderful Castle Warders. It's not a difficult job, after all – the only qualifications you need are thorough acquaintance with nine centuries of the history of Scotland, Edinburgh and the Castle; the tact, wit and grace of a high-ranking diplomat; and, most importantly, the ability to stop yourself bursting out laughing, quite a lot of the time. . .

Excuse me, which castle are we in?

Do they put the Castle up every year for the Festival?

What a swell idea building it so close to the railway station!

Did Mary Queen of Scots live here before or after her execution?

Is this where Bonnie Prince Charlie held his balls?

Why does Scotland need a crown when it hasn't got a king?

Gosh, I didn't realise there were *two* English Crown Jewels.

Do you sell replicas of the Crown Jewels in the Castle Shop?

It's so nice to be in England again.

The English are such *super* hosts.

How did they manage to build the Castle in the middle of a city?

Was Saint Margaret a saint?

Did they imprison French soldiers here during the Second World War?

Castle Warders, 1930.

Did Queen Mary's room always have a squeaky floor?
Are the Crown Jewels real?
Visitor: How old is the Castle?
Warder: Very old.
Visitor: Can you be more specific?
Warder: Yes. Very, very old.
Visitor: Why do they call it the Half Moon Battery?
Warder: Well, in the old days, they used to keep chickens up there at night.
Visitor: Why do they have a lone piper at the end of the Tattoo?
Warder: Well, it would be a bit difficult to put a full military band on top of the ramparts.
Visitor: Is this Holyrood Castle?
Warder: No, Edinburgh Castle.
Visitor: So where's Holyrood Castle?
Warder: It's Holyrood *Palace.*
Visitor: Oh, so it's got a palace *and* a castle?
Warder: Will you excuse me for a moment? I want to tear my hair out.

Mary Queen of Scots was Marie Stuart's daughter, and she was beheaded by Elizabeth II.

King James VI was hidden in the wall for two weeks after he was born. . .

The Castle was built by St Margaret in 1603.

A visitor emerging from the Great Hall, having been shown the *luggie-hole* or spy-hole, was heard to remark that they had problems with slugs making holes in there.

Visitor: (*pointing to view across the Firth of Forth*) Is that Holland over·there?

Warder: If it is, madam, the tide has just brought it in.

Visitor: (*at the Ticket Office*) A day return to Glasgow, please.

Two Canadian ladies insisted they had been told by a guide that Winnipeg could be found in the Great Hall. After some investigation it turned out that the guide had told them to have a look for the "*widden pegs*" in the hammer beam roof.

EDINBURGH EVENING NEWS
THURSDAY, MAY 18, 1939

CASTLE TELESCOPE

Fair visitors using the telescope erected beside Mons Meg at Edinburgh Castle. A two minutes' look costs a penny.

(Scotsman Publications)

"I can see Holland from here."

Mary, Queen of Scots and former Secretary of State for Scotland Malcolm Rifkind compare notes on statecraft at a book launch.

In the War Memorial building, designed by Sir Robert Lorimer in 1924 and occupying the site of the medieval church of St Mary, a piece of the Castle Rock rises dramatically through the stone floor, and was left there to enhance the power and austerity of the architect's vision. The fragment is the highest point of the Castle Rock. After this was explained to one visitor, she asked if the rock had come up after the floor was laid.

Was Scotland involved in the Second World War?

Who was Scotland fighting in the last war?

Visitor to Warder in War Memorial: I'm finding this guide-book *very* difficult to follow. **Warder:** I'm not surprised. It's the guidebook to Holyrood Palace.

A former Superintendent of the Castle could not restrain himself from bursting into gales of laughter when he saw an American gentleman wearing the loudest tartan jacket he had ever seen.

Warder: I take it you're just a bit fond of the tartan, then?

Visitor: Yes indeed, sir. I couldn't decide which tartan to choose from the book of samples, so I asked them to make my jacket up from patches of *all* of them.

Are these the same Crown Jewels as the ones in the Tower of London?

What time is the one o'clock gun fired?

Just after the one o'clock gun went off one day, a visitor was examining the clock situated next to the gun.

Visitor: Is this a nautical clock?

Warder: What makes you think it's a nautical clock?

Visitor: That's obvious. It's only got one hand.

Warder: Actually, sir, it's got two hands, and it's a perfectly ordinary clock. It's five minutes past one.

Visitor: Why is the gun fired at one o'clock?

Gunner: It's not fired at one o'clock, it's fired at 12:60.

Visitor: Why is the gun fired at one o'clock?

Gunner: This is Scotland, don't forget. A twelve o'clock gun would be far too expensive.

Visitor: Why did you drain the Castle moat?

Warder: So that we could cut the grass.

A visitor en route for the Castle after leaving Holyrood Palace ended up in a housing scheme five miles outside the city centre. Apparently he was standing at the bus-stop at the bottom of the Royal Mile and noticed the words PLEASE QUEUE OTHER SIDE written on it, so he crossed the road and waited at the bus-stop opposite.

Johnny Cash once did a Christmas Show from the Castle. During his tour of the Castle prior to the gig, he popped into the Gents'

Edinburgh Castle by night. It takes Jimmy McGlumpher, Janitor, approximately two-and-a-half weeks to change all the lightbulbs.

toilet. An electrician was standing at the urinal next to him. The electrician gave Cash a long look, peeped over the urinal, then said: *"You've no got much tae sing aboot, huv ye?"*

An elderly American lady visiting Queen Mary's Room evidently got the legend of the baby being lowered out of a Castle window a bit muddled. She asked the warder if the baby had survived. Indeed, yes, madam, the warder replied – and whatsmore, the baby went on to become King James VI of Scotland, and King James I of England. The lady peered out of the window at the road hundreds of feet below, and turned round with a look of amazement on her face, saying *"Gee, it must have been one hell of a baby to have survived such a long fall!"*

Visitor in Queen Mary's Room: Could you explain what the mark 'E' is?

Warder: It's a really big tent where you hold parties or shows outside, isn't it?

"Do they put this up every year for the Festival?"

Glossary

gubbed	smacked in the gob
gob	cakehole
cakehole	mouth
kip	sleep
nabbin	stealing
castle	very big building
skoosh	a dawdle
a dawdle	something very easy
Tam	Thomas
hame	home
Hogmanay	old year's night
old year's night	new year's eve
widden	made of wood
Tattoo	military show or display
nippers	children
tae	to
Firth of Forth	estuary of the River Forth
gee	jings
jings	gosh
gobsmacked	amazed

Staff Sergeant Tam McKay, MBE, exhausted after a hard day's work. His normal working day commences at 12.58pm and concludes at two minutes past one.

The Cadies and Witchery Tours support the one o' clock gun millennium exhibition

How to make
Paper planes

How to make and fly
Paper planes

Nick Robinson

p

This is a Parragon Book
This edition published in 2004

Parragon
Queen Street House
4 Queen Street
Bath BA1 1HE, UK

ISBN 1-40544-028-7

Produced by Haldane Mason, London

Printed in China

Contents

An Introduction to Paper Planes 6
A Brief History of Flight 8
How and Why Planes Fly 12
Making Your Own Planes 15
Flying Competitively 19

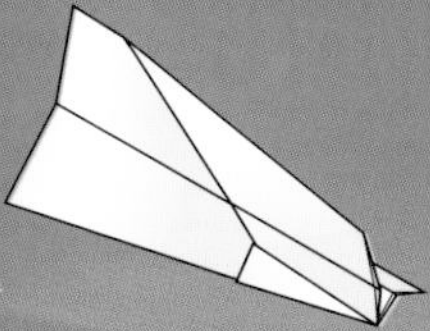

Classic Designs 23
Classic Dart 24
Hawk Dart 26
Classic Glider 30
Keel Plane 32

Modern Designs 37
Barnstormer 38
Triplane 42
Norton Flyer 46
Renishaw 48

Space Age Designs 53
Seed Floater 54
Space Fighter 56
Roller Blade 58
Whizzer 60

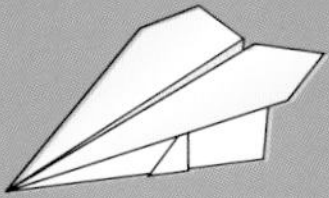

Glossary of Aviation Terms 62

Index 63

Acknowledgements 64

An Introduction to Paper Planes

Paper planes are fun to make, and making them is not only an exciting hobby but it is also one that could lead to greater things. In this introduction, Chris Edge, who holds the current world record for the longest flight of a paper plane, explains what you do once you have perfected the designs in this book.

The first step would be to get together with some friends and to see who has managed to make the best design.

When it comes to a flying competition, there are really only two choices available to you: to see whose plane flies the furthest (known as a distance competition) or to see whose plane flies for the longest time (known as a duration competition).

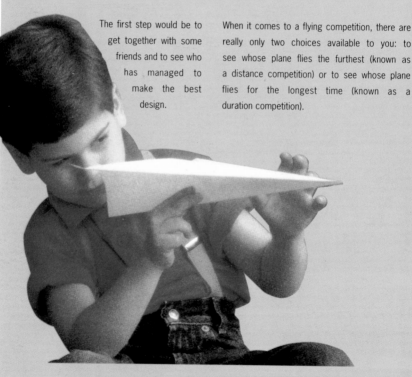

Distance competitions are comparatively easy to arrange. All you need is the use of a long room, such as a school hall. Agree on the number of flights each of you will make, mark a line on the floor and take turns to launch your planes from behind that line. As each plane lands, mark its position on the floor.

Duration contests are a little more difficult to organize because you need a high-ceilinged room, such as a sports hall. Again, agree on the number of flights each of you will make and use a stopwatch to time the plane from the moment it is thrown until the moment it lands. The plane that is in the air the longest time is the winner.

I have been mainly involved in duration competitions, and I am currently joint world record holder for the longest indoor flight with a paper plane. The record time – 20.9 seconds – was set in July 1996 in an aircraft hangar at Cardington, Bedfordshire, and it beat the previous record, which had been held for many years by American Ken Blackburn. The plane I used was a simple design, similar to many of those in the book, but I have perfected it through trial and error and some science for more than two years.

Both distance and duration contests enable you to experiment with different designs. One of the most appealing aspects of making paper planes is that you can work quickly, and if they don't work, you can just throw the paper into the recycling bin and

start again. In just a few minutes you could find that you have a world-beating design.

When you are beginning to make paper planes for a competition, bear the following points in mind. First, start with a proven design – many of the planes shown in this book are ideal. Make your planes carefully, taking trouble to fold the paper exactly as shown and starting again with fresh paper if you make a mistake. When you are making the folds, make sure they are crisp by running your fingernail along them. Sharp, neat folds will help the plane to fly. When you have finished making the plane, do a few gentle test throws and adjust the wings to see if you can improve the flight pattern. Then try some harder throws, but continue to make small adjustments to the design.

I always look forward to duration contests. I never know if the planes I will be making are going to be world beaters, but it's great fun trying. Who knows? You may find yourself folding a record-beating plane and, like me, you may end up on television.

Good luck and good throwing.

Chris Edge, London

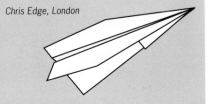

A Brief History of Flight

Although the history of manned flight is well known, no one knows for certain where or when the first paper airplanes were flown. They may well have been discovered in Ancient Egypt when papyrus was first discovered.

Paper kites are known to have been made in China over 2000 years ago, but the Greek philosopher Aristotle (384–322 BC) was the first to write down his theories of how and why things flew, although he got several things wrong.

The Italian polymath Leonardo da Vinci (1452–1519) thought that the up-and-down movement of a bird's wings was the key to flying, and he developed plans for what is known as an 'ornithopter'. We now know that this type of aircraft is not practicable, although working toys are possible. He also drew diagrams of what must have been a type of helicopter many hundreds of years before the real thing took to the air. He is thought to have experimented with parchment planes to help work out the principles of flight.

Another three hundred years passed before the English scientist Sir George Cayley (1773–1857) developed what were to become the basic principles of flight as we know them. He experimented with a number of gliders and helicopters and realized the importance of tilting the wings slightly upwards to make a plane more stable by creating a dihedral angle (see page 18). His work on

A Malayasian kite and its maker.

FIG. 4. — Croquis de Léonard de Vinci.

Drawings from the sketchbook of Leonardo da Vinci, 1508

making something that was heavier than air fly might well have been ignored by a sceptical public but for the invention of the manned balloon by people such as the French Montgolfier brothers. They used paper to make hot air balloons, and their first manned balloons, which flew in 1783 were made from cloth lined with paper.

The Aeronautical Society of Great Britain was formed in 1866, and at about the same time the German Otto Lilienthal (1848–96) and his brother were developing gliders capable of carrying a man. They discovered that wings with a curved surface had much more lift than those with flat surfaces. Lilienthal also made the first rudimentary rudder, but he was killed in 1896 during a test flight. An Englishman, Percy Pilcher had

flown in a Lilienthal glider, and he extended his work to include a wheeled undercarriage. He was in the process of designing an aero-engine when a tail failed, causing his death.

The first 'proper' flight of a real airplane was made in America by the Wright brothers on 17th December 1903 at Kitty Hawk, North Carolina, and it is possible that they may have seen and used paper airplanes. To this day, the best way of learning about the basic principles of flight is to experiment with sheets of paper.

The primitive biplanes gave way to high powered monoplanes in the late 1930s. During this exciting period the American John Northrop (1895–1981) used paper

The Wright brothers attempting a precarious landing

airplanes to test his ideas for flying winged aircraft. Those humble paper airplanes may well have played a small part in the eventual development of the Stealth bomber!

The Second World War led to a massive surge in the development of flight technology. From 1939, when biplanes were still in common use, aircraft developed into rocket- and jet-powered designs, capable of near supersonic flight. German scientists in particular explored many strange and advanced designs, including delta wings and asymmetrical designs. After the war the Americans developed many of their ideas, leading to the first supersonic flight by Charles 'Chuck' Yeager (b. 1923) in 1947 flying a Bell X-1 The speed of sound is 331m (1087ft) per second at sea level. This

speed is known as Mach 1. Twice the speed of sound is Mach 2 and so on.

Since 1947, airplanes have become faster and flown higher. The first practical VTOL (vertical take-off and landing) airplane was developed in England during the 1950s and is still in use today in the form of the Harrier jump jet. As the race for space began, planes flew to the outer edges of our atmosphere to learn how a design might work in space as well as in our own atmosphere. The NASA space shuttle is the end result of these early experiments and is a perfect combination of airplane and space craft. Designs are currently being created for larger space-going aircraft that may one day take people to distant planets.

NASA space shuttle 'Discovery' lifts off

How and Why Planes Fly

When we talk about something flying, we mean that it stays in the air for a reasonable time and behaves in a predictable way. There are two types of flight: powered (with an engine of some kind) and gliding. Paper planes fall into the second category! Luckily for us, the same principles that allow a powered airplane to fly also apply to paper airplanes. We can also use paper to explain these principles.

If you drop a sheet of paper to the floor, it twists and turns in a random way. Technically, this type of flight is called unstable. If we form the paper into the shape of a cone using sticky tape or a staple, the flight pattern changes dramatically. It now falls smoothly to the floor and will always fall in the same direction. The flight is more stable and predictable. The more tightly you roll the cone, the faster it will fall because it can slip through the air more easily.

If you drop the cone and a sheet of paper at the same time, the cone will land first, because it meets less air resistance. The main factor that creates resistance is having a bulky shape, although the density of the object (how solid it is) has an effect as well. A streamlined shape will create less resistance and so fly more smoothly. This is why fast cars and airplanes have smooth profiles: they can slice through the air more

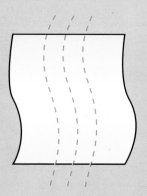

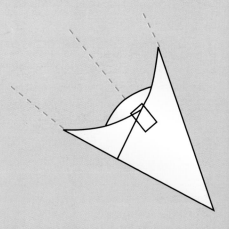

easily and meet less resistance. We can easily design our planes so that they are streamlined, but they also need to stay in the air longer than the cone does. To do this, we must create lift.

Experiments by the early pioneers showed that we can provide lift by putting a slight curve in a wing. This is explained by Bernoulli's Principle, which says that air pressure around a surface decreases as the speed of the air increases.

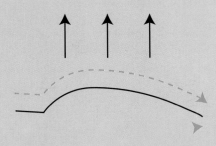

If we make a curve in the paper, air flowing over it will have to move faster over the top of a curved wing, because it has further to travel. This will create a lower air pressure on the upper surface and the wing will tend to rise. This is how we create lift. You can test this principle by holding a strip of paper with the short end near your mouth. If you blow over the top of the paper, it rises. This is because the increase in speed lowers the air pressure, creating lift.

A powered airplane will use an engine to reach speeds that give it enough lift to stay in the air. Because a paper plane is quite slow, (and we can't easily add a curve to the wing), it cannot stay in the air for much longer than 20 seconds in the best of conditions. We must make the best use of this time.

The amount of lift is also affected by the dihedral or the angle at which the wing meets the air. This is known as the angle of attack. A shallow angle provides the most lift, which is why airplanes take off and land at a gentle angle. If a wing meets the air at a steep angle, the lift will reduce until it is less than the force of gravity trying to pull it down again. When this happens we say the airplane is stalling. We want our plane to meet the air at the correct angle. This will be different for each design.

Stability in flight

For distance flights, we want our plane to fly in a fixed direction, whereas for the maximum time in the air, a gentle curve is better. In order to achieve either of these targets, the plane must not change the way in which it flies – it must be stable. In a real aircraft the pilot uses control surfaces, such as the rudder and aileron, to control the plane's stability. There are three possible ways in which a plane can turn.

Roll

If one wing goes down as the other goes up, the plane will roll. The pilot uses the aileron (*see* Glossary) to prevent rolling. On a paper plane, we adjust the angle of the wings.

Pitch

If the back of the plane falls as the nose rises (or vice versa) the plane will pitch. The pilot uses the elevators (*see* Glossary) to prevent pitching. On a paper plane, we adjust the paper at the back of the wings.

Yaw

If one wing moves further forward as the other moves backwards, the plane will yaw. The pilot uses the rudder to prevent yawing.

On a paper plane, we adjust the paper at the back of the body or the fuselage.

Although we can make some adjustments, the basic flight pattern is determined by the point around which the plane balances, which is known as the centre of gravity. If we suspended a plane by a single thread, it would balance, but only if the thread were attached at the centre of gravity. This point is determined by the final arrangement of the layers of paper. If the centre of gravity is correct, the plane will make a successful flight more often than not. Tests have shown that the ideal centre of gravity is towards the front of the plane. Most paper planes therefore have more paper at the front to make this the heavier end.

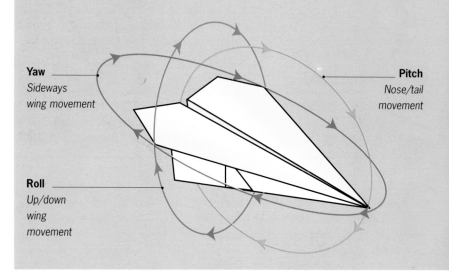

Yaw
Sideways wing movement

Pitch
Nose/tail movement

Roll
Up/down wing movement

Making Your Own Planes

**Paper is one of the simplest materials to work with.
It is cheap and widely available, and you can choose from a huge range
of colours and patterns. Most paper planes are made from rectangles
(although some use a square), and we can find suitable paper almost
everywhere we look. Photocopy paper is ideal, and you can buy packets
of it very cheaply. Most paper-folders are always on the look-out
for free samples and make good use of leaflets that may be
pushed through their letterboxes.**

When we make paper planes, we should use fresh paper of medium weight. Thicker paper works nearly as well, but might not fly very well if the model is too heavy. Thin paper can lose its shape when you launch it. Paper that has been left in the open for a long time can absorb moisture from the air and becomes 'floppy', and this prevents it from flying very well. Cheaper types of paper, such as 'rice' or 'sugar' paper are suitable for trial runs, but not for the real thing. Once you have mastered the folding method, you might want to look for some brightly patterned paper for a really special plane. You can always decorate it yourself with pencils and crayons.

If a design starts with a square, you can either use origami paper or cut your own. Specialist paper comes in a variety of exciting finishes and can give your plane a very professional look, but it can be expensive. Making squares from rectangles is very easy and you can then use the same type of paper for all your designs.

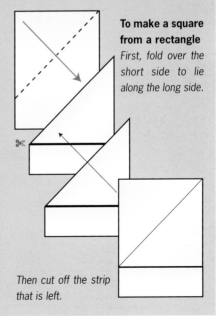

**To make a square
from a rectangle**
*First, fold over the
short side to lie
along the long side.*

*Then cut off the strip
that is left.*

15

The section of paper left over is almost the same shape as an American dollar bill. Paper plane experts like Stephen Weiss have invented a number of paper planes designed to use this shape. Why not see if you can invent one of your own?

Folding technique

When you start folding it's a good idea to use a table or other flat surface to fold on. If you are new to paper-folding, you should also stop between folds and look at the next diagram. Before creasing, check the paper is lined up exactly. If you get it wrong you can refold it, but the old creases may make life harder and the plane fly worse.

If a fold is easier made by turning the paper around or (with mountain folds) upside down, feel free to move it to the best position, but don't forget to return it afterwards so that it corresponds to the next diagram. Accurate folding also needs a neat rectangle (or square) to start with.

Using the instructions

The planes in this book are arranged with the easiest first, so you are recommended to fold through them in order. The diagrams show you a series of steps that end up with the finished plane. You must follow these steps in the order shown! It's also useful to look ahead to the next step each time, so you know what you are aiming for.

The first diagram will show creases already on the paper. These are always 'half-way' creases, made by folding the paper in half.

Symbols

Paper-folding diagrams use a series of standard origami symbols so that they can be read by anyone, regardless of language. The two basic creases are a valley fold, indicated by a dotted line, and a mountain fold (sometimes called a 'peak' fold), indicated by alternating dots and dashes.

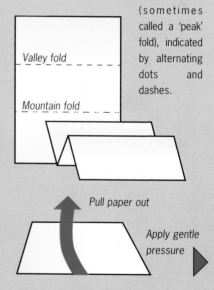

Valley fold

Mountain fold

Pull paper out

Apply gentle pressure

Other common symbols include 'pull the paper out', 'turn over the paper' and 'apply gentle pressure'.

Once you become familiar with the symbols, you will be able to make origami designs from anywhere in the world. If you invent your own plane, use the same symbols to make some instructions and send it to the British Origami Society whose address is at the end of this book.

Creating your own designs
The best way to create is to experiment with basic designs. Change the position of a crease and see how it affects the finished plane. Add extra folds, miss out folds – you don't have to follow the diagrams! Keep an open mind – some quite unlikely looking designs fly very well. Your plane doesn't have to be a typical glider, it might be a UFO or a Stealth bomber. Try to be different: you might want to make something that spins like a frisbee or a helicopter – the sky's the limit!

Flight adjustments
There are three major factors that affect the flight of a paper airplanes: the angle of

launch, the speed of launch and the dihedral.

Angle of launch
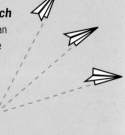
In theory you can launch the plane in any direction from down at the floor to straight up in the air.
In practice, however, each plane will have quite a limited range of angles if you want the best flight. Start by launching it forwards and slightly down, then note the flight pattern and try again with a slightly different angle. Try a wide range of angles to see which is best for your plane.

Speed of launch
Some planes fly best when launched slowly, others need a faster launch. Experiment to find the best.

Top ten tips for folding paper planes.
1. Try to find somewhere quiet so you can concentrate.
2. Set aside 'folding time' so you won't feel rushed.
3. Use a table or flat surface to fold on.
4. Make sure your hands are clean.
5. Fold slowly and carefully, making sharp and accurate creases.
6. Look ahead to the next diagram to see what you're aiming for.
7. Try not to put in 'extra' creases – they will affect the flight.
8. Never launch your plane towards anybody.
9. Don't give up if it doesn't fly properly.
10. Be prepared to experiment.

Dihedral

A paper plane is likely to roll, pitch or yaw or any combination of the three, but the biggest problem is often the pitch. We can control this by adjusting the dihedral or angle of the wings relative to the horizontal.

To give our planes dihedral, we fold the wings so that they both point upwards slightly. As one wing is lowered, the lift on the other wing is reduced, causing the plane

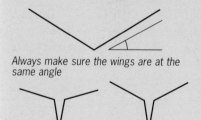

Always make sure the wings are at the same angle

Try different dihedrals for each design

to move back to a more stable position. The angle of the wings will vary for each design When altering the dihedral, always try to make sure both wings have the same angle, or the plane will tend to roll.

As you might expect, these three factors affect each other. For instance, increasing the dihedral may mean you have to launch more slowly. After a while, you will learn to predict how this happens and adjust accordingly. Be patient and try to work out what is happening during the flight.

Fine tuning

Small changes to the trailing edge of the wings can have a large effect on the flight. Try to curl the paper very gently each time, in case it makes things worse! By deliberately making large curls, you can turn the plane into a barnstorming model, which performs spectacular aerobatics.

Weight

Some planes will work better if they are made from large sheets of paper, others are better made from small sheets. If the paper is too light, it will be blown by the wind too easily. If it is too heavy, it may not fly at all. The only way to find out is to experiment.

Height

If your plane is a glider rather than an acrobatic barnstormer, it will work better if you launch it from high up, such as from a bedroom window. Make sure you don't attempt to launch yourself!

Flying Competitively

Two main categories are recognized internationally: time aloft and distance. Many competitions extend this list to include a category for acrobatics and design, but the event centres around the 'big two'. Since the early days of competition both time and distance have steadily been improved upon, and they currently stand at 20.9 seconds in the air and 58.8m (193ft) distance.

The fragile nature of paper flight means that competitions must be held indoors where there are few air currents. Launches made outdoors might produce artificially good or poor results depending on how much wind was blowing that day and in what direction!

Various techniques and theories have been developed for each category.

Time aloft

The basic principle is to throw/launch the plane straight upwards as high as you can. It will then – ideally – begin a slow, circling descent. You will be limited by the height of the ceiling and the width of the area, so it's unlikely you will break any records unless you are in a large indoor stadium of some kind. You also have to be quite flexible to throw straight upwards – try it!

Your design should be adjusted so that as soon as the plane reaches its highest point, it immediately levels out. Any height lost will mean a shorter time in the air. Once it has levelled out, your plane should have a slight imbalance so that it starts to turn in a wide circle. Ideally, this circle will be a few feet smaller than the width of the arena.

Professional paper plane makers will make minute adjustments to their basic design to try to get the widest possible turning circle. The end result will need a slice of luck, since the paper will never behave the same way twice.

Distance

The distance in question is measured from the place where you launch the plane to the point where it first touches the ground. You will only get good results if your plane is trimmed to fly in a straight line. If it flies in a circle it may well travel a long way, but may not land very far away (as the crow flies). There are two ways to achieving long distance – the missile approach and the gliding approach.

The missile approach

This is quite a crude method, involving mostly brute force. You choose a streamlined design, then hurl it as fast as possible. Since you could do the same with a screwed-up ball of paper, many contests don't allow anything that looks too much like a missile.

The gliding approach

This is where you use the plane's natural flight characteristics to achieve distance. Some competitions have a category in which you release the plane from a fixed height – in other words, you don't give it any forward thrust. This allows children to compete on the same basis as adults, because physical strength isn't an issue.

The mixed approach

In practice, the most successful contestants will use strength to get the plane started, then allow it to glide for the remainder of the distance. If you launch a plane too quickly, the wings may buckle and reduce both stability and lift. Remember, speed and angle of launch affect each other.

Preparation is the key

If you want to enter a contest, you must put in plenty of practise! You need to be reasonably fit to compete with the best and practise will build up your muscles; you'd be surprised how much your arms can ache after a few hours enthusiastic launching! As well as being fit, you must know how to adjust your design for the best result. You will only have a few attempts in a contest, so it's vital you can watch your first flight, work out what needs changing and then make those changes.

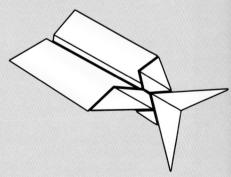

Current record holders are (at the time of writing)
Time aloft

Guinness World Record	20.9 seconds set by Chris Edge & Andy Currey 28 July 1996
Guinness British Record	20.9 seconds set by Chris Edge & Andy Currey 28 July 1996
Origami Record	20.9 seconds set by Andy Currey 28 July 1996

Distance

Guinness World Record	58.8m (193ft) set by Tony Fletch 21 May 1985
Guinness British Record	31.7m (104ft) set by Andy Currey 19 September 1997
Origami Record	28.7m (94ft) set by Robin Glynne 19 September 1997

If you decide to have a go at the record, you must have a clear video of your efforts; it isn't enough to have somebody as a witness – unless they are from the *Guinness Book of Records*! You will also need a room over 61m (200ft) long.

RULES

As you can imagine, there are lots of rules to abide by. Although you are allowed to used a small piece of sticky tape to hold your design together, many people try to use 'pure' origami methods. Here are the key rules from the Guinness Book of Records.

- *The record is for the duration or distance of an indoor paper airplane flight*

- *If your plane touches anything when in flight (including people, wall and roofing) that is then end of that flight*

- *The airplane must be made from one sheet of paper, using A4 or USA letter size paper*

- *The weight of the paper must be no more than 100 gsm (grams per square metre)*

- *The paper can be cut but any piece of paper cut off can't be joined back on again*

- *Standard clear sticky tape is allowed, but no longer than 3cm (1¹/₄in) on any one airplane*

- *The tape can be cut into smaller pieces but used only to hold down folds, not as a weight or to control the flight*

- *Glue is not allowed*

- *Ten attempts at the record are allowed*

- *The airplane should be flown by one person, from a reasonably fixed position. This means a long run up as part of the launch is not allowed*

- *When launching, your feet should not intentionally lift off the ground. The launch height is the height of the thrower, wearing normal footwear. No stilts!*

- *Distance throwers should not touch or cross over the launching line*

Classic Designs

To become a 'classic', like the Spitfire, a paper airplane must have stood the test of time. These designs have done just that and have been enjoyed by many thousands of people. These are simple yet elegant paper planes and you will be able to teach them to your friends.

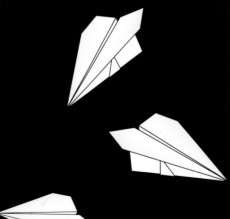

Classic Dart

This tried-and-tested design is one of the simplest to make, but also one of the best! Nobody knows how old it is, but people all over the world have made it and enjoyed flying it.

1 Start with a sheet of A4, creased in half lengthways. Fold in two corners to lie along the centre crease.

2 Take the folded edges in to the centre as well.

3 Fold the paper plane in half.

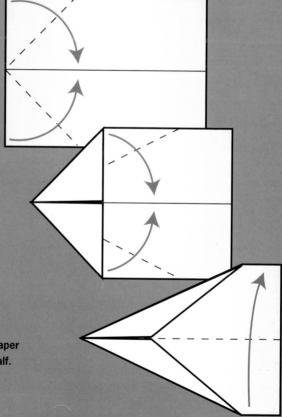

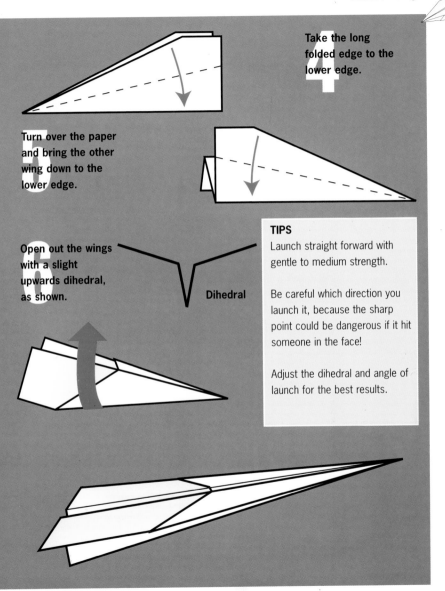

4 Take the long folded edge to the lower edge.

5 Turn over the paper and bring the other wing down to the lower edge.

6 Open out the wings with a slight upwards dihedral, as shown.

Dihedral

TIPS

Launch straight forward with gentle to medium strength.

Be careful which direction you launch it, because the sharp point could be dangerous if it hit someone in the face!

Adjust the dihedral and angle of launch for the best results.

Hawk Dart

This traditional model is a superb glider, and although it looks very complex it isn't. It will also fly without the pleats. Some folders cut off the rear of the plane and make it into a narrow tailplane. It looks good, but will not fly as well.

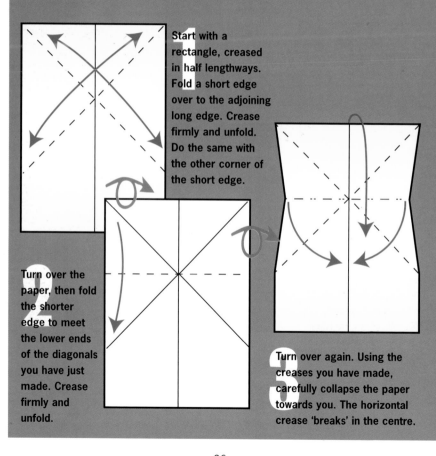

1 Start with a rectangle, creased in half lengthways. Fold a short edge over to the adjoining long edge. Crease firmly and unfold. Do the same with the other corner of the short edge.

2 Turn over the paper, then fold the shorter edge to meet the lower ends of the diagonals you have just made. Crease firmly and unfold.

3 Turn over again. Using the creases you have made, carefully collapse the paper towards you. The horizontal crease 'breaks' in the centre.

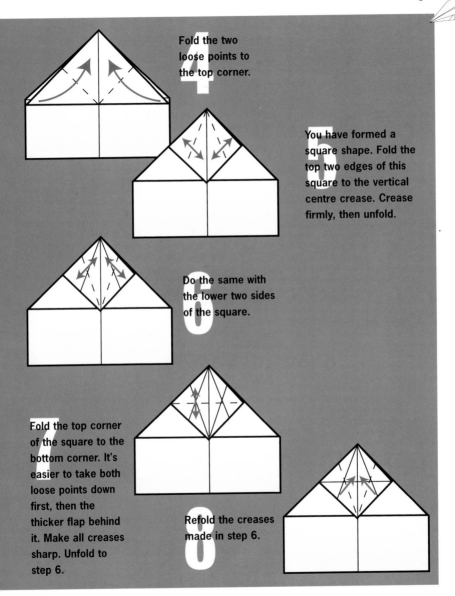

Fold the two loose points to the top corner.

You have formed a square shape. Fold the top two edges of this square to the vertical centre crease. Crease firmly, then unfold.

Do the same with the lower two sides of the square.

Fold the top corner of the square to the bottom corner. It's easier to take both loose points down first, then the thicker flap behind it. Make all creases sharp. Unfold to step 6.

Refold the creases made in step 6.

9 Carefully fold all the paper above the horizontal crease behind. Two points will form at the top of the paper. Check the next diagram to see what you're aiming at!

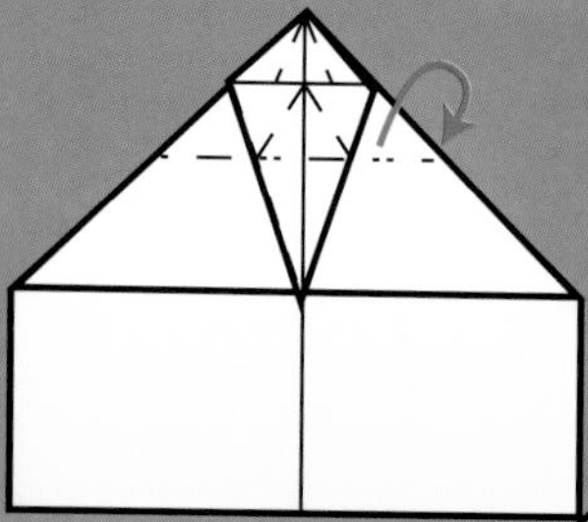

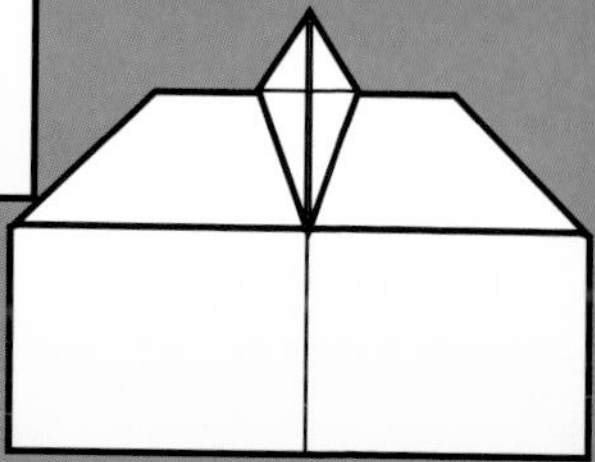

10 This is the result. Flatten all edges firmly and turn over the paper.

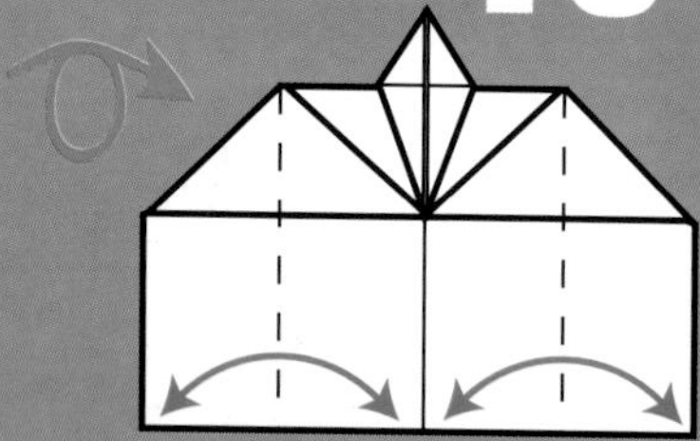

11 Fold the outside of each wing to the centre crease and unfold. Turn the paper over once more.

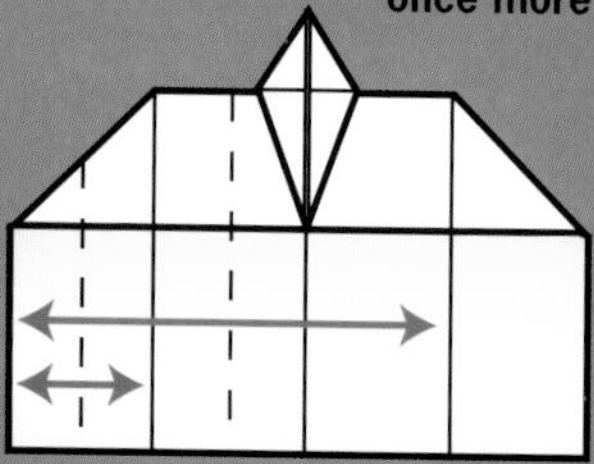

12 Add more pleats by taking the edge to the nearest crease, then to the half-way crease on the opposite side.

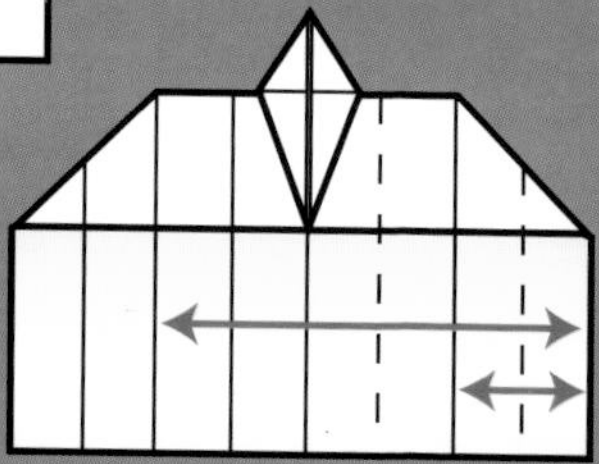

13 Do the same on the right-hand wing.

14 Open all pleats half-way out, making sure the plane looks the same on both sides.

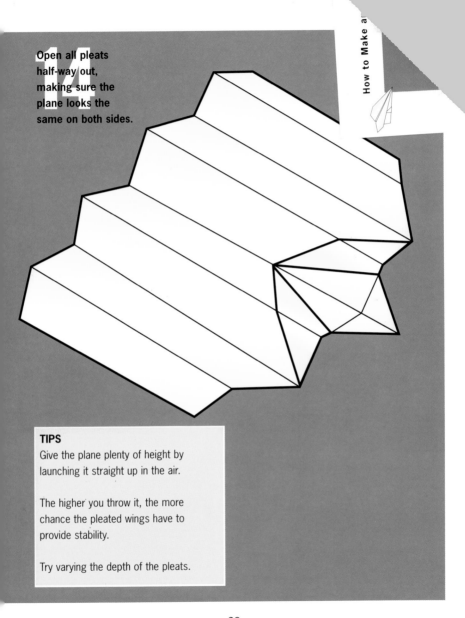

TIPS

Give the plane plenty of height by launching it straight up in the air.

The higher you throw it, the more chance the pleated wings have to provide stability.

Try varying the depth of the pleats.

Classic Glider

This is a well-known design, which represents a step forward from the classic dart. It uses a technique developed by the paper plane expert Eiji Nakamura to hold the loose fuselage flaps firmly in place. This move takes place in step 5. This is one of the designs for which there is a template supplied. Use the template as a guide to making this plane.

1 Start with a sheet of A4, creased in half lengthways. Fold in two corners to lie along the centre crease.

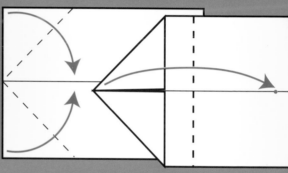

2 Fold the left-hand corner across to just short of the right hand edge. Make sure that the point lies on the centre crease. Check the next diagram to see what you're aiming at.

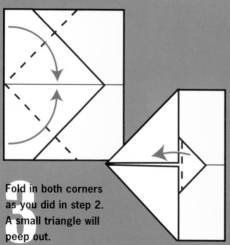

3 Fold in both corners as you did in step 2. A small triangle will peep out.

4 Fold back the triangle across the two corners. This holds the loose flaps in place when the plane is in flight.

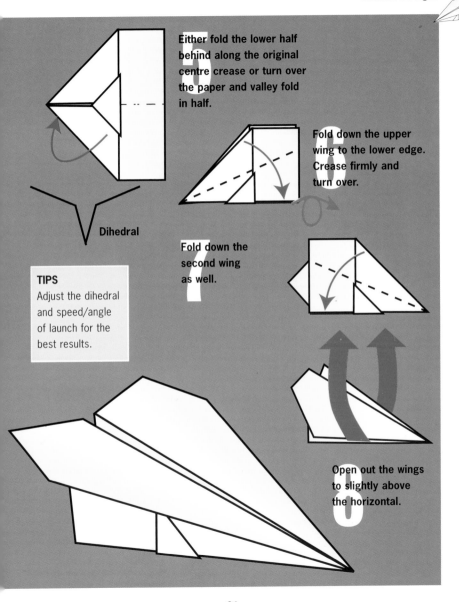

Either fold the lower half behind along the original centre crease or turn over the paper and valley fold in half.

Fold down the upper wing to the lower edge. Crease firmly and turn over.

Dihedral

Fold down the second wing as well.

TIPS
Adjust the dihedral and speed/angle of launch for the best results.

Open out the wings to slightly above the horizontal.

31

Keel Plane

This design is a variation on a traditional design and although it is very simple, it flies well. If you can fold the plane without problems, you might like to try the small variation that holds the fuselage together. This is an example of how a little thought and a few experiments can improve a basic design. Look at the other planes in this book and see if you can improve them!

1 Start with a rectangle, creased in half lengthways. Fold a short edge over to the adjoining long edge. Crease firmly and unfold. Do the same with the other corner of the short edge.

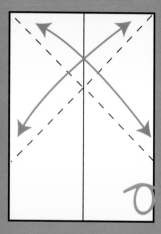

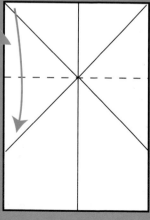

2 Turn over the paper, then fold the shorter edge to meet the lower ends of the diagonals you have just made. Crease firmly and unfold.

3 Turn over again. Using the crease you have made, carefully collapse the paper towards you. The horizontal mountain crease 'breaks' in the centre.

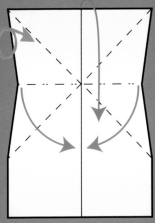

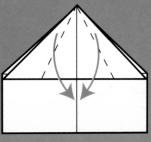

4 The top layer of paper is a triangle. Fold both outside edges downwards and in so that they lie along the centre crease.

5 Tuck the loose flaps inside the plane.

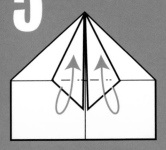

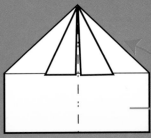

6 Fold in half behind, using the original centre crease.

7 Take the folded edge of the wing to the long edge. Because there are several layers near the fold, you may not be able to line it up perfectly.

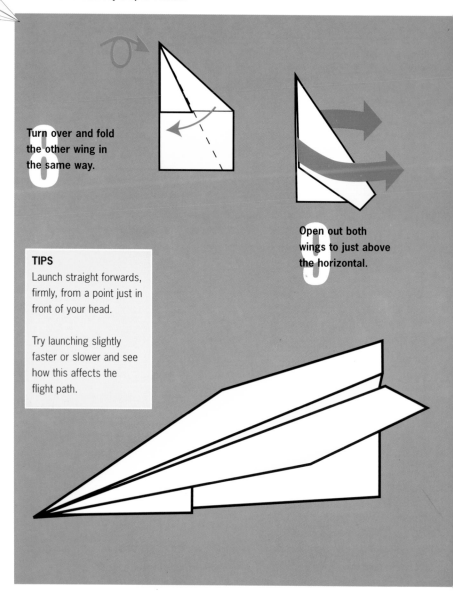

Turn over and fold the other wing in the same way.

Open out both wings to just above the horizontal.

TIPS

Launch straight forwards, firmly, from a point just in front of your head.

Try launching slightly faster or slower and see how this affects the flight path.

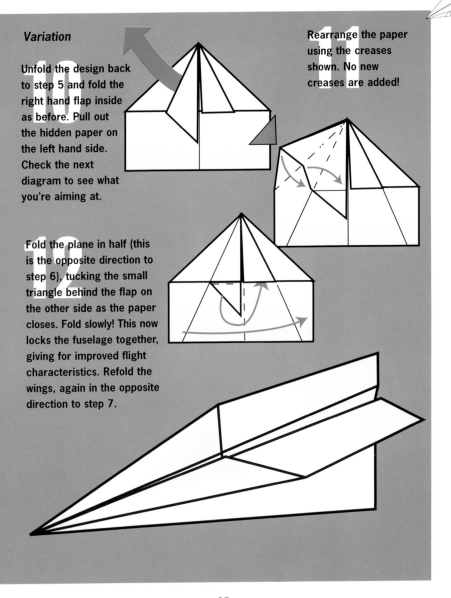

Variation

Unfold the design back to step 5 and fold the right hand flap inside as before. Pull out the hidden paper on the left hand side. Check the next diagram to see what you're aiming at.

Rearrange the paper using the creases shown. No new creases are added!

Fold the plane in half (this is the opposite direction to step 6), tucking the small triangle behind the flap on the other side as the paper closes. Fold slowly! This now locks the fuselage together, giving for improved flight characteristics. Refold the wings, again in the opposite direction to step 7.

Modern Designs

Using folding techniques discovered in the last few years, these designs represent a step forward from the traditional, classic designs. Perhaps in years to come they will become classics themselves, or like the Northrop Flying Wing (pictured left) develop into something completely unexpected, like the 'Stealth bomber'.

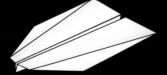

Barnstormer

This origami design by the author starts from a square rather than a rectangle. The shape of the paper causes different design problems (such as the paper becoming too thick), which can lead to unusual and exciting solutions! The variation at the end will produce 'eyes' if you start with paper that has a different colour on each side. This is one of the designs for which there is a template supplied.

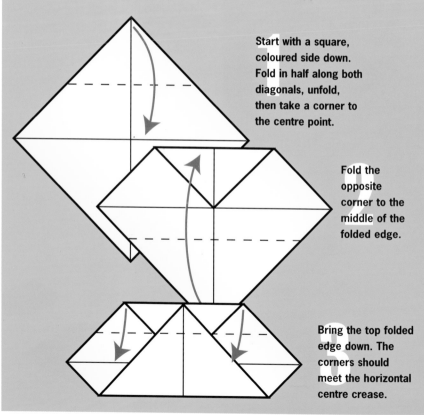

1 Start with a square, coloured side down. Fold in half along both diagonals, unfold, then take a corner to the centre point.

2 Fold the opposite corner to the middle of the folded edge.

3 Bring the top folded edge down. The corners should meet the horizontal centre crease.

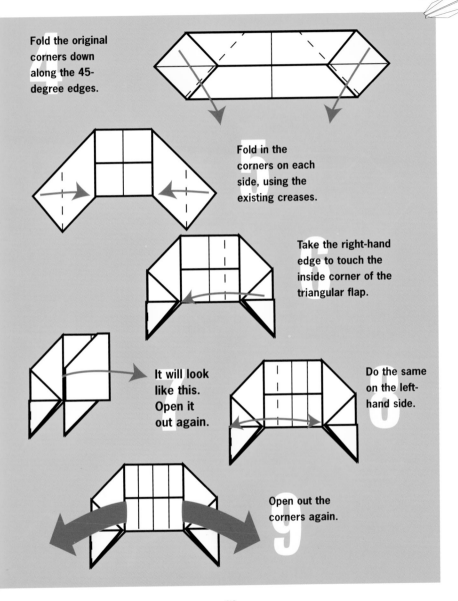

4 Fold the original corners down along the 45-degree edges.

5 Fold in the corners on each side, using the existing creases.

6 Take the right-hand edge to touch the inside corner of the triangular flap.

7 It will look like this. Open it out again.

8 Do the same on the left-hand side.

9 Open out the corners again.

39

Fold the top edge
to the central
inside edge.

10

Re-form the
creases as shown to
give shape to the
plane. Follow the
profile illustrated.

11

As a variation, fold
the rear tip of each
wing so that it tucks
under the main
body of the wing.

12

It now looks a bit
like a face.

13

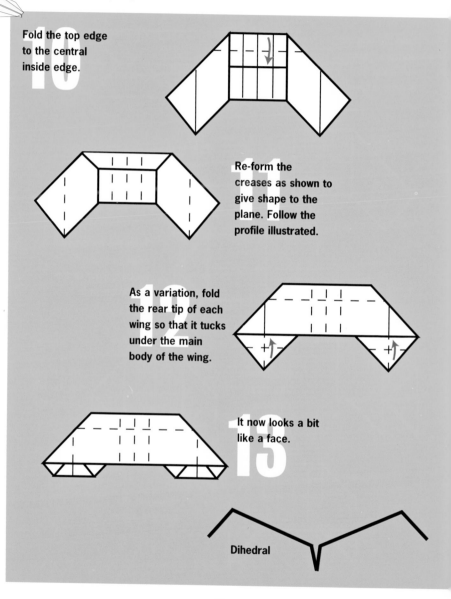

Dihedral

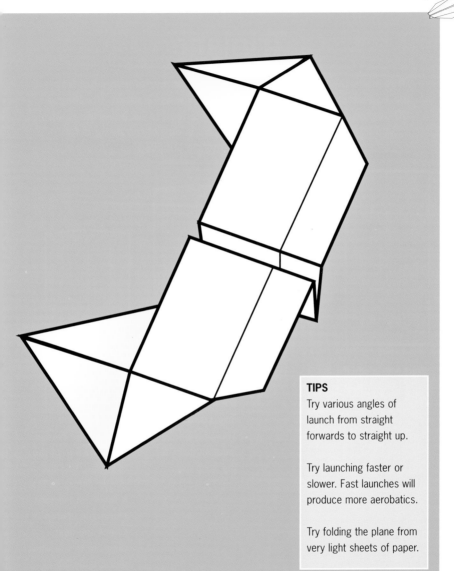

TIPS

Try various angles of launch from straight forwards to straight up.

Try launching faster or slower. Fast launches will produce more aerobatics.

Try folding the plane from very light sheets of paper.

Triplane

This plane takes its name, not from the number of wings but from the equilateral triangle that forms basic crease pattern. Creating a 60-degree crease is quite easy, but you need to be accurate when you line up the paper in step 3. This is one of the designs for which there is a template supplied.

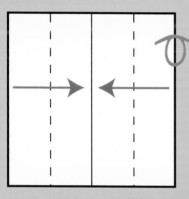

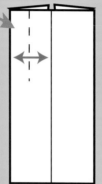

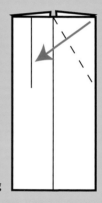

1 Start with a square, creased in half from side to side. Fold the sides to the centre and turn the paper over.

2 Fold the edge to the centre, creasing only a small section. This provides a location point for the next step.

3 Starting the crease at the middle of the top edge, fold the corner across so that it meets the crease you made in step 2. Check the next diagram to see what you are aiming at.

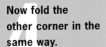

4 Now fold the other corner in the same way.

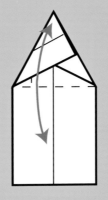

5 This is the result. Fold the top triangle down, crease firmly and unfold.

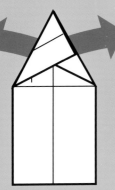

6 Open out the paper back to the square and turn it over.

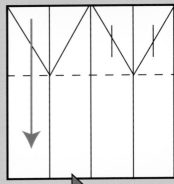

7 Fold down the top part using the crease you made in step 5.

8 Using the existing creases, swing the lower (loose) corner up to the top, flattening the top right corner as you go.

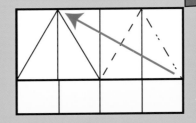

43

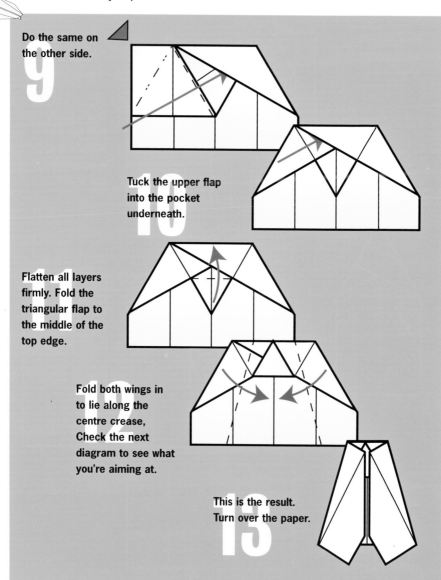

Do the same on the other side.

Tuck the upper flap into the pocket underneath.

Flatten all layers firmly. Fold the triangular flap to the middle of the top edge.

Fold both wings in to lie along the centre crease, Check the next diagram to see what you're aiming at.

This is the result. Turn over the paper.

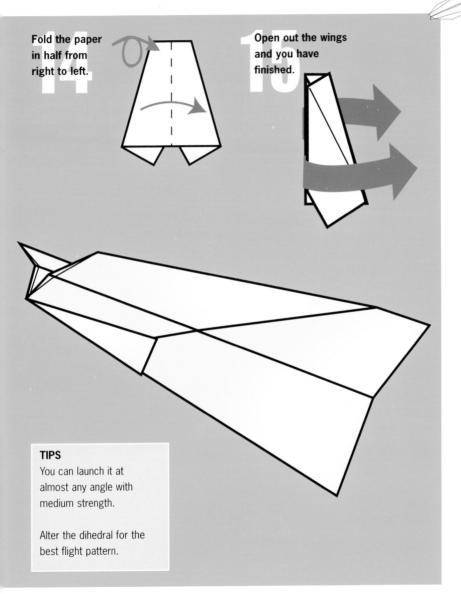

14 Fold the paper in half from right to left.

15 Open out the wings and you have finished.

TIPS
You can launch it at almost any angle with medium strength.

Alter the dihedral for the best flight pattern.

Norton Flyer

This design, named after the area in which I live, is best at slow, long-distance glides. You need to fold all creases as accurately as possible, making sure the paper is in the right place before you flatten the crease. This is one of the designs for which there is a template supplied.

1 Start with a sheet of A4, creased in half lengthways. Pinch the halfway point of this crease to find the centre of the rectangle. This pinch-mark helps locate nearly all the creases. Fold a corner to the centre point (marked with a dot).

2 Repeat with the other corner.

3 Fold the two main outside corners to the same point.

4 Fold the 'nose' corner to the same point. Try to be accurate!

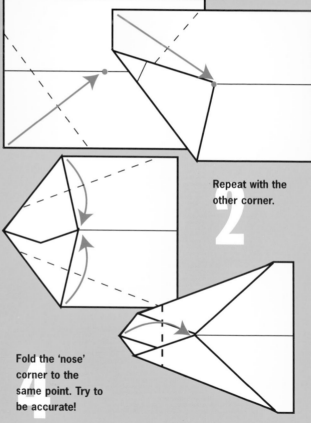

46

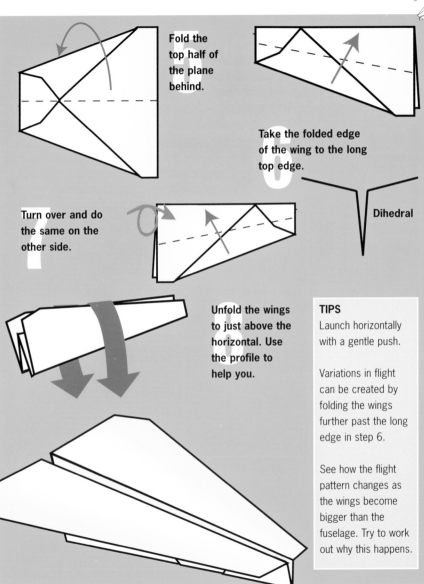

Fold the top half of the plane behind.

5

Take the folded edge of the wing to the long top edge.

6

Dihedral

Turn over and do the same on the other side.

7

Unfold the wings to just above the horizontal. Use the profile to help you.

8

TIPS

Launch horizontally with a gentle push.

Variations in flight can be created by folding the wings further past the long edge in step 6.

See how the flight pattern changes as the wings become bigger than the fuselage. Try to work out why this happens.

Renishaw

The large wing area compared to the fuselage, makes this a very stable, slow glider. Designed in a small village in Britain, the opening folds are similar to those in the Triplane (page 42) and also use 60-degree geometry. This is one of the designs for which there is a template supplied.

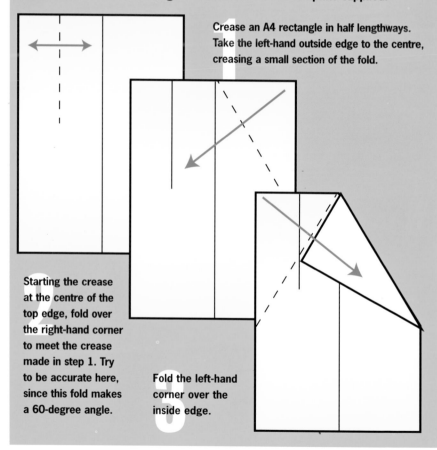

Crease an A4 rectangle in half lengthways. Take the left-hand outside edge to the centre, creasing a small section of the fold.

Starting the crease at the centre of the top edge, fold over the right-hand corner to meet the crease made in step 1. Try to be accurate here, since this fold makes a 60-degree angle.

Fold the left-hand corner over the inside edge.

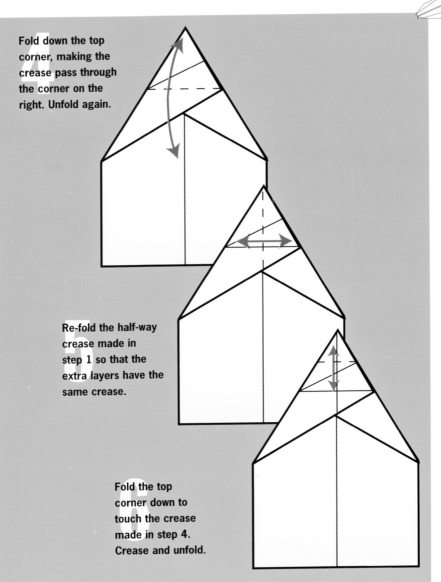

4 Fold down the top corner, making the crease pass through the corner on the right. Unfold again.

5 Re-fold the half-way crease made in step 1 so that the extra layers have the same crease.

6 Fold the top corner down to touch the crease made in step 4. Crease and unfold.

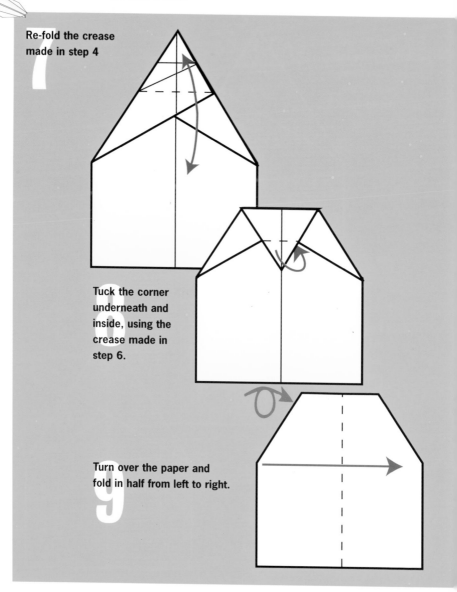

Re-fold the crease made in step 4

7

Tuck the corner underneath and inside, using the crease made in step 6.

8

Turn over the paper and fold in half from left to right.

9

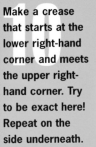

10 Make a crease that starts at the lower right-hand corner and meets the upper right-hand corner. Try to be exact here! Repeat on the side underneath.

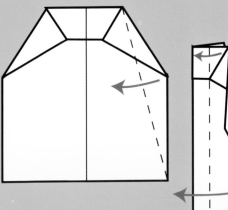

TIPS
Launch the plane straight forwards with a gentle push.

Alter the dihedral for the best flight pattern.

Dihedral

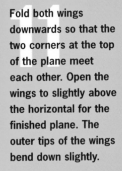

11 Fold both wings downwards so that the two corners at the top of the plane meet each other. Open the wings to slightly above the horizontal for the finished plane. The outer tips of the wings bend down slightly.

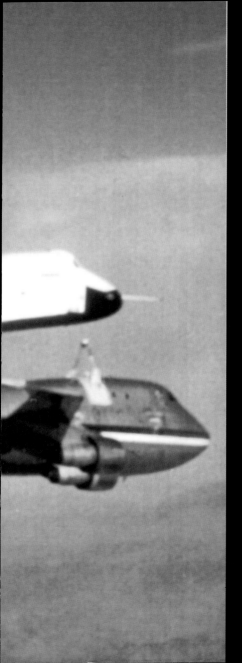

Space Age Designs

There are many ways in which a
sheet of paper can be made to fly.
Here are some examples that
spin, twist and generally point the
way forward for paper flight. Why
not use your imagination and
adapt some of the designs

presented here?

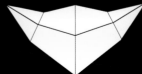

Seed Floater

The clean lines of this design were inspired by the seeds of a South American plant, which can float over 2km (1.2 miles) from the parent tree. It will need careful adjusting, but will glide beautifully when balanced. This is one of the designs for which there is a template supplied.

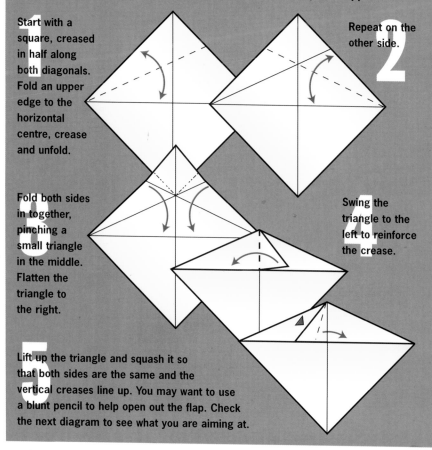

1 Start with a square, creased in half along both diagonals. Fold an upper edge to the horizontal centre, crease and unfold.

2 Repeat on the other side.

3 Fold both sides in together, pinching a small triangle in the middle. Flatten the triangle to the right.

4 Swing the triangle to the left to reinforce the crease.

5 Lift up the triangle and squash it so that both sides are the same and the vertical creases line up. You may want to use a blunt pencil to help open out the flap. Check the next diagram to see what you are aiming at.

54

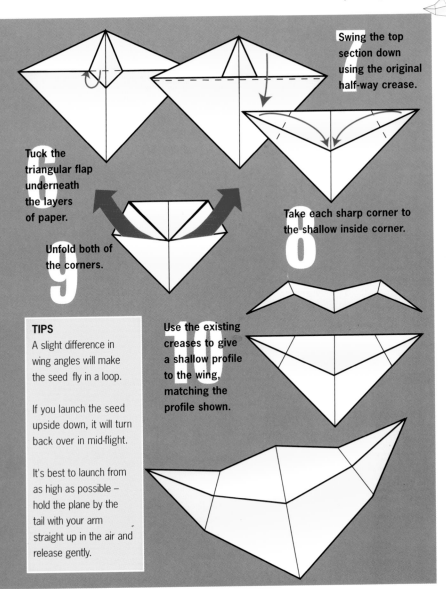

7 Swing the top section down using the original half-way crease.

6 Tuck the triangular flap underneath the layers of paper.

8 Take each sharp corner to the shallow inside corner.

9 Unfold both of the corners.

TIPS
A slight difference in wing angles will make the seed fly in a loop.

If you launch the seed upside down, it will turn back over in mid-flight.

It's best to launch from as high as possible – hold the plane by the tail with your arm straight up in the air and release gently.

10 Use the existing creases to give a shallow profile to the wing, matching the profile shown.

Space Fighter

This may be the shape of things to come if we ever colonize space. The change of angle in the wings gives the design stability when flying in our atmosphere – wings are not needed in space!

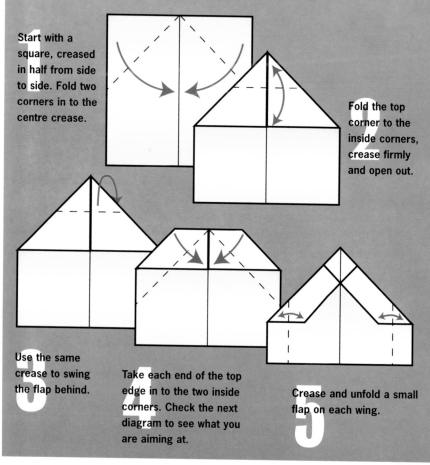

1 Start with a square, creased in half from side to side. Fold two corners in to the centre crease.

2 Fold the top corner to the inside corners, crease firmly and open out.

3 Use the same crease to swing the flap behind.

4 Take each end of the top edge in to the two inside corners. Check the next diagram to see what you are aiming at.

5 Crease and unfold a small flap on each wing.

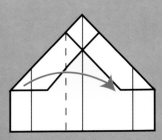

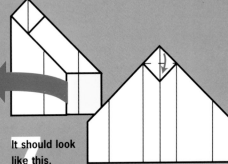

To form the main wing, fold so that the outside corner lies on an inside corner.

It should look like this. Unfold and repeat on the other wing.

Turn over the paper and fold the small square at the top in half downwards.

Using the creases you have already made, form the fuselage and adjust the wings to match the profile shown.

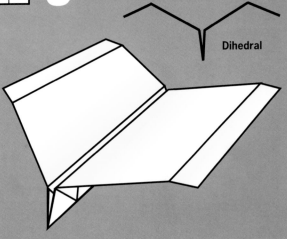

Dihedral

TIPS

Launch the plane at any speed or angle.

Adjusting the wing-tips lets you perform aerobatics and loops.

For a slow, stable glide, gently bend the rear of the wing-tips up a little.

Roller Blade

As well as designs like the Whizzer that spin round,
there are planes that twist by pitching around in a rolling motion.
Made from bright paper, this can be really eye-catching.

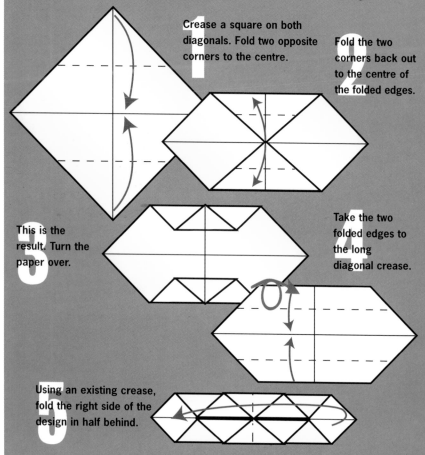

1 Crease a square on both diagonals. Fold two opposite corners to the centre.

2 Fold the two corners back out to the centre of the folded edges.

3 This is the result. Turn the paper over.

4 Take the two folded edges to the long diagonal crease.

5 Using an existing crease, fold the right side of the design in half behind.

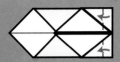

Fold over a small flap so that the right-hand corners touch the inside corners of the small triangles.

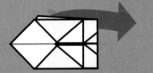

It should look like this. Release the flap of paper you folded behind in step 5.

TIPS

You launch holding near the centre with a slight downwards flick of the wrist. This starts the rolling movement and as it falls the pressure of the air perpetuates the action. Larger paper will give a slower speed of roll.

The higher you launch it from, the longer the time aloft will be, but be very careful when launching it from heights.

If you make the Roller Blade from a plain sheet of paper you can draw open eyes on one side and closed eyes on the other. As it falls and spins, you have the illusion of winking! Can you think of other tricks?

Lift the small flap upwards at right angles to the main piece of paper.

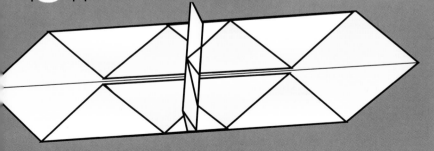

Whizzer

This traditional design isn't really a plane, but it lets you turn yourself into one! Although the folding sequence is really simple, there is a 'knack' to making it work. Don't give up too easily; once you start flying around the room, you'll want to show off your skills to your friends.

1 Start with a rectangle of thin paper about twice as long as it is wide; 15 x 7.5cm (6 x 3in) is ideal.

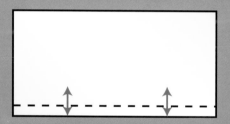

2 Fold in a small strip on any side, crease firmly and unfold.

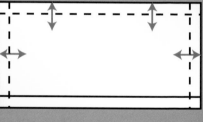

3 Do the same on the other three sides.

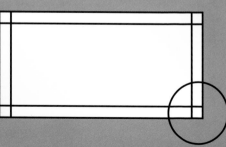

Add a small crease
to each corner,
by pinching the
paper together.

4

This is the result.

5

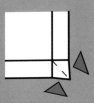

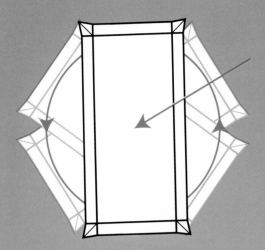

TIPS

Start to walk forwards in a straight line and as the paper starts to turn, move the front finger out of the way. As long as you move at a reasonable speed, the Whizzer will stay on your finger, spinning merrily.

If you really want to make yourself dizzy, try spinning round in a circle!

See how slowly you can move without losing the spinning effect.

When you are confident, try making the Whizzer from slightly larger or smaller paper and see how it affects the flight.

Does the Whizzer always turn one way? Why do you think this happens?

Teach some friends to fold the Whizzer, then have races!

Glossary of Aviation Terms

Aileron The hinged section of a wing that controls lateral balance.

Airfoil An aircraft wing that produces more lift than resistance.

Angle of attack The angle at which an airplane's wings meet the airstream.

Asymmetrical An airplane with wings of different shapes.

Axes The planes in which an aircraft can turn, indicated by X–X, Y–Y and so forth.

Barnstormer An airplane that can perform spectacular aerobatics.

Canard An airplane with a tail on the front rather than at the rear of the fuselage.

Centre of gravity The point at which an aircraft achieves balance.

Control surfaces The parts of an aircraft that affect its flight pattern.

Dihedral The angle formed by an aircraft's wings and the horizontal.

Elevator The stabilizer on the tail plane that is used to tilt an aircraft up or down.

Flight pattern The path through the air taken by an airplane.

Fuselage The body of an aircraft.

High-lift wing A wing that creates more lift than a conventional wing.

Laminar-flow wing A wing that creates less air resistance (drag) than a conventional wing.

Lateral control The effect of making an airplane roll (turn around its long axis).

Leading edges The front edges of an aircraft's wings.

Lift The upward force that acts on the wings.

Mach number The ratio of the speed of an aircraft to the speed of sound.

Ornithopter A type of flying machine that resembles a bird.

Pitch The up or down movement of the nose of an aircraft.

Rate of roll The speed at which an aircraft can turn around its long axis.

Roll The movement caused by one wing being higher than another.

Rudder The vertical tail plane.

Stable An airplane that flies without rolling, pitching or yawing.

Stall An uncontrolled fall to the ground when the force of gravity is greater than lift.

Supersonic An aircraft that is capable of exceeding the speed of sound.

Swept-wing An aircraft's wing on which both the leading and trailing edges point backwards.

Trailing edge The rear edge of an aircraft's wing.

Unstable An aircraft whose flight pattern varies uncontrollably.

VTOL (vertical take-off and landing) An aircraft that can take off straight upwards.

Wing tip The outer end of an aircraft's wing.

Yaw The movement caused when one wing moves ahead of the other.

Index

angle of launch 17
angle of attack 13
Aristotle 8

Barnstomer 38–41
Bell X-1 10
Bernoulli's Principle 13

Cayley, Sir George 8
centre of gravity 14
Classic Dart 24–5
classic designs 23–35
Classic Glider 30–31
competitive flying 19–21

Dart, Classic 24–5
Dart, Hawk 26–9
dihedral 18

Fighter, Space 56–7
Floater, Seed 54–5
Flyer, Norton 46–7

Glider, Classic 30–31

Hawk Dart 26–9

Keel Plane 32–5

Leonardo da Vinci 8, 9
Lilienthal, Otto 9

Montgolfier, Joseph Michel
    and Jacques Etienne 9
mountain fold 16

NASA 10
Northrop, John 9–10
Norton Flyer 46–7

origami paper 15
ornithopter 8

Pilcher, Percy 9
pitch 14
Plane, Keel 32–5

Renishaw 48–51
resistance 12–13
roll 14
Roller Blade 58–9

Seed Floater 54–5
space travel 10, 11
Space Fighter 56–7
speed of launch 17

Triplane 42–5

valley fold 16
vertical take-off and
    landing (VTOL) 10

weight 18
Whizzer 60–61
Wright, Orville and Wilbur
    9, 10

yaw 14
Yeager, Charles 10

Acknowledgements

I'd like to express my thanks to various members of the British Origami Society for advice and encouragement over the years, including Lord Brill, Edwin Corrie, Mark Kennedy, David Mitchell, Paul Jackson, Wayne Brown, Paulo Mulatinho and many others. I would also like to thank Ken Blackburn for making his vast knowledge of flight available to me; my wife for being patient when I spend far too much time on my computer; my children for keeping me humble and tired; and Penny Groom for introducing me to my publishers!

The author

Nick Robinson is a former professional origami teacher. He has visited schools, libraries, youth clubs, hospitals and many other venues, teaching origami and paper artwork. He has worked with people of all ages and physical abilities, included those with both aural and visual disabilities. His favourite origami designers include David Brill, Kunihiko Kasahara and Philip Shen.

Nick has appeared on television, radio and has written other books on the subject. His original creations have been published in 13 countries around the world. He has contributed articles and designs for the British Origami Society (BOS) magazine and has served on its council for over ten years. He prepares the worldwide web pages for the BOS and takes a keen interest in computers and the Internet. As a former professional musician, he still performs live, playing solo improvised ambient guitar.

British Origami Society

For membership details of the society, please write to;

Penny Groom
2a The Chestnuts
Countesthorpe
Leicester LE18 3TL